Making a Difference in Africa:
Advice from Experienced Grantmakers

By Rob Buchanan and Jayne Booker

With an Introduction by
Former President Jimmy Carter

D0965124

COUNCIL *on* **FOUNDATIONS**

The Council on Foundations in collaboration
with The Africa Grantmakers' Affinity Group

AFRICA
Grantmakers'
Affinity
Group

2121 Crystal Drive, Suite 700
Arlington, VA 22202
703-879-0600 • fax 703-879-0800
www.cof.org

VISION

The Council's vision for the field is of

A vibrant, growing and responsible philanthropic sector that advances the common good.

We see ourselves as part of a broad philanthropic community that will contribute to this vision. We aim to be an important leader in reaching the vision.

MISSION

The Council on Foundations provides the opportunity, leadership and tools needed by philanthropic organizations to expand, enhance and sustain their ability to advance the common good.

To carry out this mission, we will be a membership organization with effective and diverse leadership that helps the field be larger, more effective, more responsible and more cooperative.

By *common good* we mean the sum total of conditions that enable community members to thrive. These achievements have a shared nature that goes beyond individual benefits.

By *philanthropic organizations* we mean any vehicle that brings people together to enhance the effectiveness, impact and leverage of their philanthropy. This includes private and community foundations, corporate foundations and giving programs, operating foundations, and public foundations, as well as emerging giving and grantmaking mechanisms involving collective participation.

STATEMENT OF INCLUSIVENESS

The Council on Foundations was formed to promote responsible and effective philanthropy. The mission requires a commitment to inclusiveness as a fundamental operating principle and calls for an active and ongoing process that affirms human diversity in its many forms, encompassing but not limited to ethnicity, race, gender, sexual orientation, economic circumstance, disability and philosophy. We seek diversity in order to ensure that a range of perspectives, opinions and experiences are recognized and acted upon in achieving the Council's mission. The Council also asks members to make a similar commitment to inclusiveness in order to better enhance their abilities to contribute to the common good of our changing society.

437 Madison Avenue, 37th Floor
New York, NY 10022-7001
212/812-4212
www.africagrantmakers.org

The Africa Grantmakers' Affinity Group (AGAG) is a membership network of foundations that are currently funding in Africa or are interested in funding in Africa. AGAG was established as a forum for foundations to exchange information and work together in an effort to amplify current foundation funding and promote increased and more effective grantmaking in Africa to better address Africa's development challenges.

Membership in AGAG is open to both new and experienced foundations that meet the membership requirements of the Council on Foundations, but membership in the Council on Foundations is not a prerequisite for membership in AGAG.

AGAG membership services include an active e-mail list server of grantmakers, an annual meeting, learning calls and informal sessions on current issues in African development relevant to grantmaking and grantmakers. AGAG also conducts specialized research on foundation funding in Africa.

© 2007
Item #613
ISBN 1-932677-20-8

Table of Contents

A Message from Jimmy Carter

My personal involvement in Africa began 25 years ago, when, as President, I made a state visit to Nigeria and Liberia in 1978. This trip was the beginning of a long and gratifying relationship with the continent. Four years later, Rosalynn and I founded The Carter Center to wage peace, fight disease and build hope among the world's poorest people. Since then, The Carter Center has worked to alleviate suffering and advance human rights in more than 65 countries, most of them in Africa.

Over the past 20 years, The Carter Center has supported initiatives in Africa to improve health, strengthen democracy, prevent and resolve conflicts and increase food production. However, the Center's efforts would have been impossible without the financial support from foundations and corporations that recognized the enormous potential of Africa's human and natural resources, as well as the importance of this region to the rest of the world.

The Carter Center has joined forces with the Bill & Melinda Gates Foundation, for example, in the fight against Guinea worm disease — a debilitating affliction that affects the most vulnerable populations in 13 African countries. The Center also partners with the W.K. Kellogg Foundation to assist the Government of Mozambique in increasing citizen participation in shaping a vision for sustainable development. These two examples illustrate the current spirit of grantmaking in Africa.

When I visit Africa, I talk with women and men, leaders and ordinary citizens, from every part of society, about the challenges they face and their hopes for a brighter future. In a world where the gap between the rich and poor continues to widen, we can provide no greater gift than to support the aspirations of Africa's people for a better tomorrow. I have seen people transform their lives against all odds and under the most trying of circumstances, and private philanthropy has a crucial role to play in support of the positive changes that Africans are making.

This introduction to grantmaking in Africa highlights opportunities, challenges and rewards for grantmakers. It also provides practical advice and examples of successful initiatives. I hope this book will encourage more foundations and corporations to become active in Africa.

Jimmy Carter

Acknowledgments

The authors are grateful to the following individuals for their contributions to this book:

Bisi Adeleye-Fayemi, *Co-Founder, The African Women's Development Fund in Ghana*

Akwasi Aidoo, *Director of The Ford Foundation's Special Initiative for Africa*

Edward Ahnert, *President, ExxonMobil Foundation*

Chris Allan, *Associate Director, Global Greengrants Fund*

Jennifer Astone, *Director, Firelight Foundation*

Carmen Barroso, *Director, Population and Reproductive Health, The John D. and Catherine T. MacArthur Foundation at time of interview, currently with International Planned Parenthood Federation*

Reverend Canon Ogé Beauvoir, *Program Associate, Trinity Church*

Carol Berde, *Executive Vice President, McKnight Foundation*

Catherine Bryant, *Program Officer, Izumi Foundation*

Ellie Clelland, *Program Officer, Global Catalyst Foundation*

Brenda Colatrella, *Senior Director, Worldwide Product Donation Policy and Programs, Merck & Company, Inc.*

Randall Cooper, *Chairman, Cogitare Foundation*

Larry Corley, *Executive Director, Family Care Foundation*

Ed Diener, *Resident Counsel, David and Lucile Packard Foundation at time of interview, currently Vice President at the Omidyar Foundation*

Dr. Linda Distlerath, *Vice President of Global Health Policy, Merck & Co.*

Valentine Doyle, *Program Officer, Lawson Valentine Foundation*

Bamikale Feyisetan, *Program Officer, David and Lucile Packard Foundation*

Tamara Fox, *Program Officer, The William and Flora Hewlett Foundation*

Andrea Gay, *Senior Program Officer, United Nations Foundation*

John Harvey, *Executive Director, Grantmakers Without Borders*

Dyanne Hayes, *Vice President for Programs, Conrad N. Hilton Foundation*

Cornelia Higginson, *Vice President for International Programs, American Express Philanthropic Program*

Astrid Honeyman, *Programme Development Specialist, Bernard van Leer Foundation in The Netherlands at time of interview, currently with Inter-Country Peoples' Aid in Zimbabwe*

Adaora Ikenze, *Program Officer for Africa, The Global Fund for Women at the time of interview, currently with the Commonwealth Secretariat in Great Britain*

Andrea Johnson, *Program Officer, Carnegie Corporation of New York*

Kakuna Kerina, *Executive Director, Initiative for West Africa, Open Society Institute*

Larry Kressley, *Executive Director, Public Welfare Foundation*

Christa Kuljian, *Director, South Africa Office, Charles Stewart Mott Foundation at time of interview, currently with the Centre for Policy Studies in South Africa*

Don Lauro, *Senior Program Manager, David and Lucile Packard Foundation*

Casey Lintern, *Program Officer, Conrad N. Hilton Foundation*

Marc Ross Manashil, *Executive Director, The Clarence Foundation*

Gail McClure, *Vice President for Programs, W.K. Kellogg Foundation*

Charles H. McTier, *President, Robert W. Woodruff Foundation*

Chris Mkhize, *Director and CEO, Uthungulu Community Foundation in South Africa*

Don Mohanlal, *Executive Vice President, International Youth Foundation*

Joyce Moock, *Associate Vice President, The Rockefeller Foundation*

Tammy Moody, *former Program Director, Firelight Foundation*

William Moses, *Senior Program Officer, The Kresge Foundation*

Inviolatta Moyo, *Director, Community Foundation of the Western Region of Zimbabwe*

Nancy Muirhead, *Assistant Secretary and Program Office, Rockefeller Brothers Fund*

Niamani Mutima, *Director, Africa Grantmakers Affinity Group*

Monica Mutuku, *CEO, Kenya Community Development Foundation*

Abdoulaye Ndiaye, *Program Officer, The John D. and Catherine T. MacArthur Foundation at time of interview, currently with UNDP in West Africa*

Nomhle Nkumbi-Ndopu, *Director, Social Change Assistance Trust in South Africa*

Kerry Olson, *President and Founder, Firelight Foundation*

Katharine Pearson, *The Ford Foundation Representative, Office for Eastern Africa at time of interview, currently with the Center for Rural Strategies in Kentucky*

Suzi Peel, *Associate Director for Orphans and Vulnerable Children at Family Health International's Institute for HIV/AIDS and former Firelight Foundation Advisory Board Member*

Dr. Gordon Perkin, *Senior Fellow in the Global Health Program, Bill & Melinda Gates Foundation*

Dr. Daniel Robbins, *Chairman, J.F. Kapnek Charitable Trust and Pediatric AIDS Foundation, Zimbabwe*

Dr. Michael Sinclair, *Vice President, The Henry J. Kaiser Family Foundation*

Dr. Kevin Starr, *Trustee and Project Liaison, Mulago Foundation*

John Taylor, *Executive Vice President, Merck Company Foundation at time of interview, currently on the faculty of Lehigh University*

Katherine Turner, *Chief Research Officer, The Advisory Board Foundation*

Miriam Were, *Chairman, UZIMA Foundation in Kenya*

Duncan Whiteside, *President, Maidstone Foundation*

The authors wish to thank especially *Niamani Mutima, William Moses, Akwasi Aidoo, Andrea Johnson, Don Lauro, Kale Feyisetan,* and *Abdoulaye Ndiaye* for reviewing various drafts of this book and offering their helpful comments. The authors are also grateful to *Char Mollison,* Vice President for Constituency Services at the Council on Foundations, for her encouragement and support; *Fumiyo Layman,* the Council's International Programs Fellow, for her research assistance; and *Stephen Dau,* International Programs Communications Coordinator, for his editing suggestions.

In addition, the Council on Foundations is grateful to the following funders for their grant support to the Council's International Programs Department, without which this book would not have been possible:

American Express Company
Atlantic Philanthropies
Ford Foundation
W.K. Kellogg Foundation
Bernard van Leer Foundation
Charles Stewart Mott Foundation
David and Lucile Packard Foundation
John D. and Catherine T. MacArthur Foundation
TOSA Foundation

All African proverbs throughout this book come from *The Wit and Wisdom of Africa, Proverbs from Africa and the Caribbean* by Patrick Ibekwe, Africa World Press, 1998.

CHAPTER 1

Introduction

"Looking carefully is understanding."
(Ovambo proverb from Angola and Namibia)

This book is a joint effort of the International Programs Department of the Council on Foundations and the Africa Grantmakers' Affinity Group (AGAG). Although the authors hope that grantmakers already working in Africa will find the book a useful resource, we view the primary audience as boards, managers and staff of grantmaking organizations that may be interested in starting a new program or expanding an existing one in Africa. Some of the ideas in this book may also be relevant to making grants in the United States and other regions of the world.

Because media coverage of Africa pays little attention to events that indicate positive trends and the efforts that Africans are making to meet the challenges they face, many grantmakers may be wary of engaging on the continent. American interest in Africa has declined since the end of apartheid in South Africa. Yet, recent developments on the continent point to opportunities to support important fundamental changes that are occurring there. Today, there are more democratic and civilian governments in Africa than at any time in the last century. Civil society and community organizations are taking advantage of the Internet to share problems and seek solutions across national borders. As a result, there are many opportunities for U.S. foundations and corporate grantmakers to take advantage of their resources, flexibility, independence, convening powers and influence to support institutions both within and outside of Africa that play a role in the continent's positive developments. While acknowledging the challenges, this book seeks to present a more balanced picture of Africa by highlighting the many opportunities for grantmakers to become involved in the continent in effective and rewarding ways.

This book is based on interviews with 50 foundation and corporate officers from 33 foundations. Interviews were conducted with CEOs, executive directors, trustees, program officers and managers responsible for developing, implementing and assessing grantmaking programs in many of Africa's 54 countries. These grantmakers reflect a broad diversity of geographic and programmatic interests as well as different approaches to grantmaking. Some of the foundations interviewed have many decades of experience in Africa while others are relative newcomers. The Rockefeller Foundation, for example, has funded in Africa since 1914, and the Carnegie Corporation of New York began funding there in 1925. The Firelight Foundation, Global Catalyst Foundation and United Nations Foundation, on the other hand, were all established since 1998.

The sizes of the foundations interviewed run the gamut from mega-foundations like the Bill & Melinda Gates Foundation, the Ford Foundation and the David and Lucile Packard Foundation with assets in the multi-billion dollar range to small foundations like the J.F. Kapnek Charitable Trust and the Cogitare Foundation with assets of less than $5 million. Approximately 60 percent of those interviewed represent private foundations, including both family and independent, with endowments as the source of their grantmaking budgets. Others represented are public charities that raise funds from individuals, corporations and foundations to fund their grantmaking activities. Corporate grantmaking programs and corporate foundations were also included in the study. A church program and a membership organization provide some additional grantmaking perspectives.

The foundations surveyed also represent a variety of different approaches to grantmaking in Africa. Some prefer to fund charitable programs that provide food, medicine and care for orphans, while some seek to strengthen religious institutions. Others support community activists and grassroots organizations that are working for social change, while still others fund advocacy programs aimed at bringing about national or international policy change. And, some grantmakers support the strengthening of public institutions such as universities and ministries of health.

Grantmaking portfolios in the sample were as diverse as the grantmakers themselves. Grant sizes ranged from just $300 to $20 million. Similarly, the percentage of dedicated Africa grants to total foundation grants ranged from a low of 1.5 percent to 100 percent in a few cases. The 33 foundations and corporations interviewed make grants in 39 of greater Africa's 54 countries that fall within the scope of this book. The greatest number fund in South Africa (18), followed by Kenya (15), Tanzania (13), Nigeria (11), Uganda (11), Zimbabwe (10), Ghana (9) and Mozambique (9). The top focus of grantmaking in Africa among the interviewees was health, nutrition and population, followed by education, the environment and human rights. See Appendix III for a listing of the foundations interviewed for this book along with the specific countries in Africa and sectors in which they are funding.

While the foundations interviewed represent a cross-section of all grantmakers funding programs related to Africa, there are many others. The Foundation Center's 2004 database lists 165 U.S. grantmaking organizations with programmatic interests in Africa. According to studies of international grantmaking trends conducted by the Foundation Center and the Council on Foundations, grantmaking by U.S. foundations for international purposes has grown dramatically from $680 million in 1994 to $3.1 billion in 2002. At the same time, the portion of grants going directly to recipients in the large part of Africa south of the Sahara Desert has declined steadily from 24 percent in 1990 to 18.9 percent in 2001 in spite of the widening development gap between Africa and the rest of the world. While the interest and commitment of grantmakers to international giving continues to grow, many funders still shy away from making grants to Africa. Specific concerns about funding in Africa, and how experienced grantmakers deal with them, are addressed in Chapter 8. Chapter 2 highlights the many good reasons to fund there.

Regardless of the countries where grantmakers choose to fund, their issue focus, approach or size of their grants, the common denominator of all the organizations interviewed is that they share an enthusiasm for working in Africa as well as a commitment to enhancing the effectiveness of their grantmaking programs. They are glad to share their experience and insights in hopes of inspiring other grantmakers to become engaged with the challenges and opportunities offered by Africa and its people.

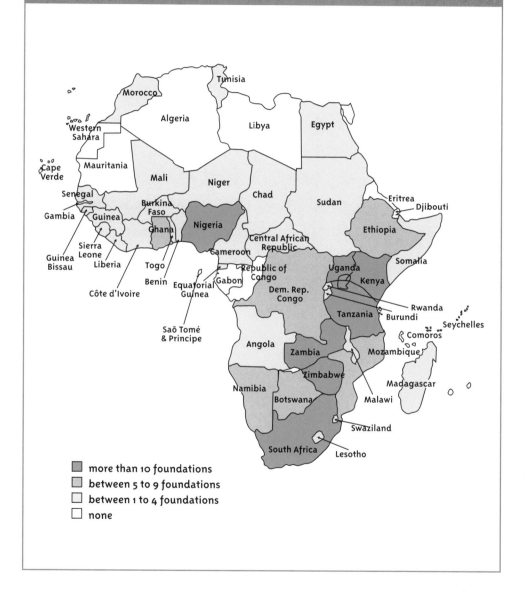

Geographic Distribution of Foundation and Corporate Grants in Africa

(based on the 33 grantmakers interviewed for this book)

- ■ more than 10 foundations
- ■ between 5 to 9 foundations
- □ between 1 to 4 foundations
- □ none

CHAPTER 2

Six Reasons to Fund in Africa

"As you give, so you receive." (Ugandan proverb)

Africa's Importance to the U.S. and the World ⁀ Abundant Human, Natural and Creative Resources ⁀ Many Opportunities for Partnership ⁀ High Impact: With a Little, You Can Do a Lot ⁀ Compelling Needs ⁀ Professional Growth and Learning

Why do foundations and corporate grantmakers choose to fund in Africa? What lies behind grantmakers' commitment and enthusiasm for their work in Africa? The answers to these questions vary depending on the individual and the foundation. However, the following six themes were touched on by many of the experienced grantmakers interviewed for this book:

Africa's Importance to the U.S. and the World

Africa is the world's second largest continent encompassing more than one-quarter of the world's countries with 13 percent of its population. Moreover, Africa is the historical birthplace of humanity and the cultural heritage of more than 38 million Americans.

The process of globalization is affecting Africa just like other regions. Minerals, diamonds, coffee, tea, gum Arabic, plant and animal biodiversity used to manufacture pharmaceuticals, animal hides and cotton are among the important commodities Africa supplies to the world. U.S. trade with Africa, while modest compared with other regions, is expanding. Fourteen percent of U.S. oil consumption is currently supplied from Africa, a figure that is expected to rise to 25 percent by 2015. U.S. exports to South Africa alone exceeded exports to Russia in 2001. In recognition of Africa's growing economic importance to the United States, the U.S. Congress in 2000 enacted the Africa Growth and Opportunity Act to support the changes under way on the continent to more transparent governance and stable market-oriented economies.

Eminent Africans provide global leadership in critical areas of international cooperation, racial reconciliation, peace-building and human rights. African winners of the Nobel Peace Prize have included three South Africans: Albert John Lutuli, an early leader of the African National Congress (ANC); Bishop Desmond Tutu, an anti-apartheid activist; and Nelson Mandela, ANC leader and South African President. Ghana's Kofi Annan, another Nobel Peace Prize winner, has been elected twice to serve as Secretary General of the United Nations, succeeding Egypt's Boutros Boutros-Ghali in that post. Uganda's highly regarded Olara Otunnu, who headed the International Peace Academy in the 1990s, currently serves as the U.N.'s Under Secretary General and Special Representative for Children and Armed Conflict. And Graça Machel, a former education minister and first lady of Mozambique, was recognized worldwide as a forceful advocate for women and children in her own right long before her marriage to Nelson Mandela.

In addition, Africans contribute significantly to world culture. Africa's rich literature, music, dance, film and other arts are becoming more widely known and admired due to technologies that are bringing a globalized world closer together. African writers like Nigeria's Wole Soyinka, Egypt's Naguib Mahfouz and South Africa's Nadine Gordimer are internationally acclaimed winners of the Nobel Prize for Literature. An African film industry is evolving. And, celebrated musical artists like Senegal's Youssou Ndour and South Africa's Miriam Makeba, to name only two, have achieved world-class status. Beyond these more famous names are countless more who give artistic expression to Africa's many vibrant cultures.

Beyond what Africa and its people are giving to the world, Africa is important for another reason. Lessons learned from Africa can inform and strengthen the work of U.S. grantmakers domestically. Carol Berde of The McKnight Foundation, which funds women's empowerment projects in three African countries, comments: "The issues are not totally different overseas than they are in Minnesota. We are more informed about international developments that affect the large number of immigrants that have settled in Minnesota. We have a larger frame of reference in which to understand the problems of poverty, disadvantage and gender discrimination that are the core of our domestic work. Our domestic programs are stronger today as a result of our international grantmaking."

Despite its importance, "Africa has all but fallen off the global radar screen," comments Kakuna Kerina of the Open Society Initiative for West Africa, "with the exceptions of the oil, gas and mining sectors and the HIV/AIDS crisis." In a globalizing world linked ever more closely through commerce, communications, culture and travel, it is short-sighted to ignore opportunities to support the positive changes that are occurring in Africa or to turn a blind eye to the challenges confronting the continent. Cornelia Higginson of the American Express Philanthropic Program, comments, "In the end, we will all be deeply affected by the situation in Africa. The implications of poverty, unrest and illness are enormous. We are deluding ourselves if we think AIDS in Africa doesn't affect us."

Abundant Human, Natural and Creative Resources

Many of Africa's 54 geographically varied countries are rich in both natural and human resources. Minerals such as copper in Zambia, diamonds and platinum in South Africa and gold in the Congo; energy supplies like the oil deposits of Nigeria, Chad, Angola and Sudan; and the rich animal and plant biodiversity used for pharmaceuticals from Gabon and Rwanda are but a few of the continent's immense natural treasures. Sudan is a major supplier of gum Arabic. And cobalt, used in the production of computers, is a principal export of the Democratic Republic of Congo.

A major impact of the colonial legacy has been to direct the economies of African countries toward the export market rather than production for local consumption. The challenge is to mobilize Africa's considerable human, natural and creative resources in ways that will also enable cottage industries and small-scale enterprises to contribute to local and regional development. Regional African governmental organizations like the Economic Commission of West Africa (ECOWAS) and the Southern Africa Development Council (SADC) are working to promote regional economic integration and development.

> "Africa is not rich in money, and its riches beneath the earth have often brought more grief than gain. But there is one asset we possess in abundance and which has never failed once we resolved to use it — our capacity for solidarity. Call it Africa's 'comparative advantage.' Acting in solidarity, Africa has already overcome droughts, floods, global economic upheaval, colonialism and apartheid. In every case, we emerged the stronger for it. So it can be with AIDS."
>
> – Dr. Mamphela Ramphele, Managing Director, The World Bank

Africa's greatest resource is its 850 million people. Included among them are many talented and educated professionals — teachers, doctors, scientists and experts in every field, many of whom have created, built and managed non-governmental development organizations that are driving the continent's development. In many parts of Africa, women, who already bear primary responsibility for food production, generating household income and childcare, also take on leadership roles in nonprofit organizations.

Moreover, Africans are tremendously creative. One has only to look at the rich textiles produced by highly skilled weavers in Mali, Ghana and Senegal; the intricate goldsmithing skills of artisans in the Côte d'Ivoire; or the fine wood work reflected in the elaborate carved doors of Ethiopia or Tanzania to appreciate the artistry and creativity of Africans. Forced to do a lot with a little, Africans are also creative at finding ways to use the resources at hand to maximum advantage. Gail McClure of the W.K. Kellogg Foundation notes, "The people are really ready to do something about their own development; there's a great natural and human resource base. There are competencies, skills and riches that are there, that may not be apparent. Africans are humanists, they care about people; they put people first." Daniel Robbins of the J.F. Kapnek Charitable Trust agrees: "There's incredible potential. They are phenomenally gifted and talented people, people with skills and dedication."

Similarly, Adaora Ikenze, formerly with The Global Fund for Women and now with the Commonwealth Secretariat, points out that "Every continent has had its time of renaissance. It's time for Africa. We now have two or three generations of articulate, educated people who are willing to contribute to their future. We have a responsibility to allow this generation to fulfill its greatest potential."

Many Opportunities for Partnership

Africa offers a wide spectrum of potential partners for grantmakers ranging from community-based organizations (CBOs) and African non-governmental organizations (NGOs, which function much like U.S. nonprofits) to government agencies, universities, research and policy institutions and religious groups. As a result, there are many options available for grantmakers to implement their funding programs in Africa.

Throughout Africa, informal community-based organizations have traditionally existed for protection, mutual aid and self-help. These include village associations, women's groups, youth organizations, agricultural work groups and others. They are a part of the African social fabric. Independence in the 1960s and 70s saw the beginnings of a more organized indigenous NGO sector in some countries, often as mechanisms for foreign interests, including American foundations, to support civil society organizations rather than governments.

Since the early 1990s, with the widespread shift away from state-dominated societies and centrally managed economies toward greater democracy and market-driven economic policies, sub-Saharan Africa has witnessed the emergence of a rich and varied civil society sector. Some African NGOs have a local focus while others are organized at the national level. Still others have a regional multi-country focus and some are working Africa-wide. African NGOs are supplying most of the talent, energy and hard work in support of the continent's development and transformation, often without external assistance. In addition to Africa's CBOs and NGOs, African governments, universities and regional organizations like the U.N.'s Economic Commission for Africa, the African Union (formerly the OAU), the Southern Africa Development Council (SADC), the Economic Commission for West Africa (ECOWAS) and the East African Economic Community offer partnership opportunities for external funders around development needs.

Beyond African organizations, there are many relief and development-oriented NGOs based in the United States and other countries that operate programs in Africa, often in partnership with indigenous African civil society organizations or government agencies. The full range of potential partnerships for funding in Africa will be discussed in chapters 5 and 6. For a grantmaker interested in funding in virtually any African country in any particular sector, suitable partners exist. "Anything you fund in America, you can fund in Africa," points out Gail McClure of the W.K. Kellogg Foundation.

Funders active in Africa confirm that African NGOs and community-based organizations can make strong partners by contributing their knowledge of the local context, traditional approaches to solving problems, access to communities and ability to mobilize them for specific activities, as well as talented and dedicated community leaders. However, while these organizations work diligently to address problems at the grassroots level, they typically lack financial resources, some technical skills and access to international networks, which grantmakers can provide.

African NGOs struggle for financial viability with sources of funding varying greatly from country to country. A study by the Johns Hopkins Center for Civil Society Studies reveals that, in South Africa, 32 percent of nonprofit sector funding is derived from charging fees for services, 44 percent comes from the public sector and 24 percent from corporations, foundations and individual donations. In Kenya, fees account for 81 percent of funding with only 5 percent coming from the public sector and 14 percent from private philanthropy. By comparison, in the United States, the Hopkins study reports that 57 percent of nonprofit revenues derive from fees and other charges, 31 percent from public sources and 13 percent from philanthropy.

Committed leaders and dynamic organizations, often at the vanguard of change in their societies, provide an additional reason to fund in Africa. Development expertise and technical skills are also available from highly trained Africans in every field. The International Planned Parenthood Federation's Carmen Barroso, formerly with the John D. and Catherine T. MacArthur Foundation, summed it up this way: "The potential is fantastic in terms of a vibrant civil society. The energy and local talent are enormous."

High Impact: With a Little, You Can Do a Lot

Grantmakers who have not funded in Africa are often deterred by the continent's huge needs, feeling that their relatively small amount of funding cannot possibly make a difference. While having a significant impact on Africa's problems of hunger, illiteracy and HIV/AIDS, for example, would require a large commitment of resources well beyond the scope of most foundations, it is also possible to have an impact on a specific community or organization with modest grant resources.

In Africa, project costs are generally much lower than costs for similar activities in the United States. However, when high tech equipment or services are purchased the costs may not be lower. But on the whole, favorable exchange rates result in small U.S. dollar grants converting into comparatively large amounts in local currency. Moreover, the impact of grant dollars can be multiplied because core funding for a project or organization often attracts additional human resources in the form of volunteers resulting from a strong tradition of volunteerism in the NGO sector.

Grantmakers funding in Africa concur that well-timed, small-dollar interventions can improve local conditions and the lives of people, at least temporarily, with a directness and immediacy often not apparent in domestic U.S. grantmaking. "We've seen it work — small dollars targeted to the right groups can change children's lives in an incredible way," points out Tammy Moody, former program director at the Firelight Foundation, which funds community programs to support children affected by HIV/AIDS. Marc Manashil of the Clarence Foundation, which links donors with sustainable community initiatives, echoes this view: "There is a tremendous amount that can be done with small amounts of money. Think of all the lives you can impact." And according to Andrea Johnson at the Carnegie Corporation of New York, "Dollar for dollar, we can probably make a greater difference in the lives of individuals in Africa than we can in the lives of Americans, where money is in greater supply."

Compelling Needs

"In looking at the world, you cannot *not* work in Africa," declares Gordon Perkin of the Bill & Melinda Gates Foundation. Whether in the fields of education, healthcare, population, the environment, agriculture, governance or any other, the needs of Africa are vast and compelling. Of course, it is Africans themselves who are most acutely aware of their needs and who are working diligently and creatively to address the challenges they face, with or without external support. But U.S. grantmakers can play an important role in supporting them. The Rockefeller Foundation, for example, has a long history of funding agricultural research by Africans to develop improved seed varieties and other technologies that have significantly increased food production on the continent. Similarly, the Rockefeller Foundation joined with The Ford Foundation, the Carnegie Corporation of New York, and the John D. and Catherine T. MacArthur Foundation in 2000 to form the Higher Education Partnership to address the needs of Africa's universities. Other examples of how U.S. foundations and corporations are working with Africans to address critical needs are described in Chapter 9.

Adaora Ikenze of the Commonwealth Secretariat notes, "Africa is the continent with the largest number of disenfranchised people — educationally, socially, economically." According to the World Bank, Africa has the highest concentration of the world's poorest countries. Of the 42 nations listed by the World Bank as highly indebted poor countries worldwide, 34 (80 percent) are located in Africa. In 12 African countries, more than half the population survives on less than $1 per day. Average life expectancy in the region is only 49 years. "Look at the statistics," urges The Clarence Foundation's Marc Manashil, "Nineteen of the top 20 countries for children's mortality under age five are in Africa." And, close to 30 million people in Africa are infected with HIV/AIDS. Even in South Africa, the continent's wealthiest nation, apartheid's legacy of income disparities and limited opportunity mean that many black South Africans are no better off than their counterparts in many of Africa's less affluent societies.

Beyond these basic human needs are many others like strengthening democracy and transparency in governance, building civil society institutions that can affect public policy, supporting hospitals and research laboratories, training university teachers and administrators, catalyzing the emergence of a thriving private sector and expanding Africa's communications infrastructure beyond urban centers. "Everything is urgent in Africa. Whatever the area, there are critical issues that need to be dealt with now," comments Abdoulaye Ndiaye, formerly of the John D. and Catherine T. MacArthur Foundation and now with the United Nations Development Programme (UNDP) in West Africa. Chris Allan of the Global Greengrants Fund put it this way: "You find it all in Africa in greater proportion."

> *"Sub-Saharan Africa has 71 percent (28.5 million) of the population living with HIV/AIDS but only 11 percent of the world's population. In some sub-Saharan African nations, up to a third of adults are estimated to be infected with HIV. South Africa has the largest number of people living with HIV/AIDS in the world (5 million)."*
>
> *- HIV/AIDS Policy Fact Sheet, The Henry J. Kaiser Family Foundation, July 2002*

Professional Growth and Learning

A recurring theme that emerged from this book's interviews is the high degree of professional growth and learning that come from making grants in Africa. Many noted that the experience of funding in Africa contributes to their foundation's understanding of community development, cross-cultural dynamics, partnerships and other issues that enhance their grantmaking activities in other places, including the United States. Working with talented and inspiring African partners and developing relationships with them over time was cited repeatedly as especially gratifying for grantmakers. A number of funders describe their work in Africa as a transformative experience, tremendously rewarding on both a personal and professional basis.

Typical are comments from Randall Cooper of the Cogitare Foundation, who says: "I take enormous pleasure from our work in Africa. If you make grants in Africa, you are bound to make a difference in human lives." Andrea Johnson of the Carnegie Corporation of New York expresses a similar view: "I consider myself very fortunate to be working in Africa. The issues are very compelling and the unique blend of history and culture is exciting."

CHAPTER 3

The African Context: Major Trends

"Knowledge is like a baobab tree and no one person can embrace it with both arms." (Ewe proverb from Ghana, Benin and Togo)

Economic Performance and Infrastructure ∿ Health, Education and Population ∿ Democracy and Governance ∿ Peace and Security ∿ Africa-Wide Initiatives

Africa is an immense continent whose 850 million people are dispersed over 54 countries covering a landmass three times the size of the United States. Many of Africa's countries are undergoing significant transformations with improving economies, expanding democracy, resolution of longstanding conflicts and practical initiatives to enhance regional and pan-African cooperation. It is an exciting time to be engaged in Africa.

Africa is also extraordinarily diverse, a mosaic of hundreds of distinct ethnic and linguistic groups. The Democratic Republic of Congo and Egypt are no more alike than, say, Quebec and Arizona. It is important to keep in mind that African countries differ significantly one from another in addition to which important differences of culture, history and political economy distinguish each of Africa's principal regions as well as each country. Consequently, you cannot assume that experience in one African country or region is automatically transferable to another. Moreover, because most of Africa's modern boundaries were artificially drawn by colonizers without regard to tribal and ethnic realities on the ground, there can be great cultural variation even within countries. What is appropriate in one place may not work in another.

While it is not possible to explore the distinctiveness of each African country individually in this book, this chapter will endeavor to provide a general overview of major trends and developments in Africa in which grantmakers new to Africa can be engaged. See Appendix I for a listing of resources leading to information on specific countries and Appendix II for a brief discussion of regional differences in Africa.

Economic Performance and Infrastructure — Cautious Optimism

> *"Africa is a continent of great potential, undergoing intense change. The development challenges that lie ahead are daunting, but there are also grounds for optimism. Real social and economic progress is taking place and the (U.N.'s) Millennium Development Goals can still be achieved in Africa by 2015. We stand ready to do everything we can to help ensure that the continent's enormous potential is unlocked."*
>
> *- Mark Malloch Brown, Administrator of the United Nations Development Programme, UNDP Website*

High economic growth rates are fueling solid economic gains in parts of Africa, even by U.S. standards. Uganda and Rwanda achieved impressive economic growth rates in 2002 of 6.2 percent and 9.9 percent respectively. And Mozambique, coming out of decades of civil war and more recent serious flooding, achieved a phenomenal 12 percent rate of growth in 2002, one of the world's highest. Botswana, Eritrea and Niger have also demonstrated strong economic performance in recent years.

Despite these economic dynamos, the U.N.'s Economic Commission for Africa characterized the continent's overall economic performance in 2002 as "lackluster." Average economic growth of Africa's national economies slowed to 3.2 percent in 2002, down from 4.3 percent the previous year and 5 percent in the mid-1990s. A few countries like politically troubled Zimbabwe, the war-torn Democratic Republic of Congo and Côte d' Ivoire have experienced negative rates of growth.

The downturn in Africa's overall economic growth rate in 2002 reflects a number of internal and external factors: the weaker global economy, lower commodity prices, trade barriers for African agricultural products and textiles in developed countries, droughts in southern and eastern Africa, the impact of HIV/AIDS and continued armed conflict in a number of countries. A general lack of infrastructure such as roads and bridges seriously impedes Africa's development, although national and regional transportation systems do exist and are being improved in many areas. While each African country has a few wealthy elites and a middle class of varying size, the World Bank estimates that 50 percent of Africa's 850 million people live on less than $1 per day and 75 percent exist on less than $2 per day.

Agriculture is the mainstay of Africa's economy, with over 70 percent of the population — a majority of whom are women — engaged in the sector. Development efforts focusing on land tenure issues, rural credit, marketing infrastructure and the needs of small-holder farmers for appropriate low-cost technologies are resulting in some rural economic growth and improved food security in countries like Ethiopia, Mozambique and Guinea. Overall, however, agricultural productivity per capita has declined. Because of the general lack of rural economic opportunity, migration from rural to urban areas continues, exacerbating overcrowded cities and fueling a host of urban social problems. Africa's urban population has increased by 50 percent since 1980, accounting today for about 35 percent of the total population. Cairo, Egypt and Lagos, Nigeria are among the world's most densely populated and still growing cities.

Much of Africa's economic infrastructure was created during the colonial period. As a result, roads, railways and communications generally supported export economies by linking high-resource areas in the interior to ports along the coast. However, since independence national development strategies and multi-country initiatives have begun to strengthen regional infrastructure linkages in order to facilitate greater economic activity within and among Africa's countries.

Communications in Africa are improving. Cell phone use is growing rapidly, providing a boon to cell phone companies. Internet connectivity in Africa is also on the rise although the global digital divide is still felt acutely throughout the continent. Each of Africa's 54 countries has Internet access in its capital city. However, high illiteracy rates, poor land-line telephone communications, lack of electricity in many rural areas and the prohibitive cost of computers are currently limiting factors to rapid Internet expansion in Africa. According to a report by Africa Internet Connectivity, African dial-up Internet subscribers in 2002 totaled 1.7 million or about one in every 160 Africans. However, subscribers in North African countries like Egypt and Morocco together with South Africa account for 1.2 million of this figure, leaving 500,000 subscribers spread across the remainder of continent.

Health, Education and Population — Many Challenges Ahead

Just as health and education lie at the heart of American society, they also are central to African societies. There are some encouraging signs regarding the health of Africans. In sub-Saharan Africa, for instance, infant mortality — a basic health indicator — declined by nearly 15 percent between 1985 and 2000. Moreover, the percentage of children in the same region under the age of five who are immunized against measles and DPT (diphtheria, pertussis/whooping cough and tetanus) has increased dramatically since 1986. And in Uganda, the rate of growth of HIV/AIDS infections has been slowed significantly through effective education campaigns.

Though declining, under-five mortality rates in sub-Saharan African countries are still high, averaging 97 deaths per 1,000 live births with much higher rates in some countries. Every year in Africa, four million children die of treatable diseases such as acute respiratory infection, malaria and measles. Moreover, only 55 percent of Africa's population has access to safe water and sanitation facilities, with this figure even lower in rural areas.

Unfortunately, the HIV/AIDS pandemic is further straining Africa's health resources. An estimated 19 million Africans, often in their most productive years, have already died of HIV/AIDS, leaving more than 13 million AIDS orphans. Fueled by cultural norms that do not encourage the open discussion of sex, the mobility of young men in search of employment and other factors, HIV/AIDS infection rates in 41 African countries now exceed 8 percent of the population. In Zimbabwe, the infection rate has risen to 25 percent and in Botswana 35 percent.

More than half of African women and nearly three-quarters of its men are literate. However, primary school enrollment rates in Africa have actually fallen in the past 20 years with only 70 percent of boys and 50 percent of girls enrolled in primary school. With limited resources for school fees and clothing, families are often forced to choose one child for schooling, and that is most often a son rather than a daughter.

In Africa, as elsewhere, high rates of population growth can slow economic performance and improvements in living standards. The good news is that the average fertility rate in Africa is beginning to fall, but it remains among the world's highest — 5.2 children per family, reflecting in large part Africa's agricultural economy and rural population base. Africa's population grew overall by 2.3 percent in 2001 but rates vary considerably from country to country. Angola, Chad, Niger and the Democratic Republic of Congo, for instance, are experiencing substantially higher population growth rates while in South Africa, Kenya and Nigeria lower population growth is pulling down the continent-wide average.

Democracy and Governance — Encouraging Signs

Africa's European colonial powers did little to encourage or prepare their colonies for self-rule, so the post-independence path toward Western-style democracy has seen many missteps, promising starts and backsliding during the past 50 years. The challenge of governance in Africa has been to overcome the debilitating legacy of colonialism and to blend traditional patriarchal forms of community leadership with newer concepts of democratic participation, minority rights and gender equality within multi-ethnic states. There is evidence to suggest that this challenge is being met in a growing number of African states.

As the charismatic and visionary leaders of Africa's liberation struggles — Jomo Kenyatta in Kenya, Léopold Senghor in Senegal, Kwame Nkrumah in Ghana, Julius Nyerere in Tanzania, Kenneth Kaunda in Zambia and others — have passed from the scene, a new more pragmatic group of leaders has emerged — like Thabo Mbeki of South Africa, Olusegan Obasanjo of Nigeria, John Kufuor of Ghana and Abdoulaye Wade of Senegal. These leaders are committed to making an African form of democracy work, fighting corruption, creating economies favorable to growth and investment and working collaboratively on a continent-wide basis for the betterment of Africa. Africa's rapidly expanding civil society is playing an ever more important role in harnessing citizen participation and holding governments accountable. Further discussion of Africa's civil society is included in Chapter 6.

Botswana and Mauritius are among Africa's longstanding stable democracies. And in some of Africa's most populous nations — Nigeria, South Africa and Kenya — democracy is clearly on the rise. Nigeria, for instance, restored democracy in 1999 after six years of military rule. South Africa has successfully managed two presidential elections and a leadership transition in the post-apartheid period since 1994. And, Kenya ended several decades of heavy-handed one-party dominance with the election of a popular opposition candidate to the presidency in 2002.

On the other hand, Zimbabwe's multi-party democracy is facing serious challenges. Somalia, Sudan and Libya are currently among the least democratic of Africa's states.

> **"** *Africa can never go back completely to its pre-colonial starting point, but there may be a case for at least a partial retreat, a case for re-establishing contacts with familiar landmarks of yesteryear and then re-starting the journey of modernization under indigenous impetus.* **"**
>
> - Ali Mazrui, "The Africans, A Triple Heritage," BBC Publications, 1986.

Peace and Security — Real Progress

That many of Africa's most recalcitrant conflicts are gradually giving way to peaceful settlements, frequently through the diplomatic efforts of respected African leaders, is one of the most hopeful signs for the continent's future. Longstanding conflicts in South Africa, Mozambique and Ethiopia were settled in the 1990s although skirmishes continue between Ethiopia and Eritrea, the independent country that was formerly Ethiopia's northernmost province. A fragile peace accord in the Democratic Republic of Congo, brokered in 2001 by South Africa's President Thabo Mbeki, was signed by six neighboring countries involved in that country's conflict, although fighting continues in parts of the country.

The Angolan civil war ended in 2002 with national elections set for 2004. And the framework for a negotiated resolution of Sudan's decades-long conflict was also agreed to in 2002, with much work remaining on the details and implementation. That same year, a civil war in Sierra Leone ended and elections were held a few months later. Liberia's civil war came to an end in 2003 as the result of intervention by a West African multi-national force and brief U.S. military presence following the flight of that country's despotic ruler Charles Taylor. And in fragmented Somalia, a tentative peace agreement was reached in early 2004 among all of the armed groups representing clan factions in the central and southern regions of that country, which has been without a central government since 1991. Under the plan, traditional clan leaders and politicians will elect a parliament.

The history of armed conflict in Africa, draining precious resources away from human and economic development, has multiple roots — historical, ideological and political. Factors fueling conflict include throwing off colonial regimes, jockeying for political power, maintaining national integrity and accessing land and other resources. Moreover, Africa's arbitrary political map left many ethnic and kinship groups divided by national borders, forcing them into unnatural associations with longstanding rivals and culturally alien groups. A prime example is Sudan's 20-year conflict over regional autonomy and control of oil resources between culturally and ethnically distinct northern and southern regions of that country.

Another factor underlying Africa's conflicts has been ideological struggle, often fueled during the Cold War by the United States and the Soviet Union, both of which viewed Africa as a stage for "proxy wars." An example is Angola's long-running conflict, with that country's considerable oil resources at stake, between a Soviet-backed government aided by Cuban troops and a rebel movement materially supported by the United States and apartheid-South Africa. A third factor fueling conflict in African countries has been the manipulation of traditional ethnic tensions by powerful national leaders as a means of ensuring their own political ascendancy. Siad Barre's longstanding grip on a fragmented Somalia, Daniel Arap Moi's dominance in Kenya despite his own minor ethnic group and Robert Mugabe's current regime in Zimbabwe serve as examples.

That Africans are bringing so many of the continent's conflicts to an end stands as a major achievement. At the same time, the post-conflict challenges are great — reconciliation, reconstruction, demilitarization and integrating soldiers, many of whom are orphaned and uneducated children, into peaceful societies. Moreover, ongoing conflicts in Chad, the Central African Republic, Uganda and Burundi are reminders that more conflict resolution work remains to be done.

Africa-Wide Initiatives — Forward Momentum

The Organization of African Unity (OAU) was created in 1963 to uphold each member's territorial integrity as well as to foster dialogue and cooperation among Africa's leaders. Over the next 40 years, the OAU issued a series of non-binding declarations addressing topics such as human rights, child welfare, participatory government, external debt and economic growth. In 2000, the African Union was formed as a further step toward political, social and economic integration of the continent. An African Union Executive Council, a Commission and a pan-African parliament were created as well as a Peace and Security Council, an Economic, Social and Cultural Council and a Court of Justice.

Perhaps the most significant new pan-African initiative is the New Partnership for Africa's Development (NEPAD), launched in 2002 with the strong backing of South Africa's President Mbeki, Nigeria's Obasanjo and others. NEPAD is based on the conviction that only by ending its civil wars, adopting democratic and transparent forms of governance and ensuring political stability with the rule of law will Africa as a whole attract the foreign investment viewed as critical to it's economic growth. Under NEPAD's novel "peer review" mechanism, African leaders will critique the performance of fellow African governments in meeting measurable targets in specific fields such as good governance, agriculture, education and energy.

> ". . . there have been many grand plans for the
> recovery of Africa which quickly failed, mostly because
> lip service did not translate into real action. Still, there
> are reasons to be mildly optimistic about this one
> (NEPAD). It has not been imposed by outsiders but
> drawn up by some of the continent's most responsible
> leaders."
>
> — The Economist, "An African Cure for Africa's Ills," June 22, 2002

As these trends suggest, Africa is changing as new social movements, organizations, technologies and leaders emerge to play critical roles in the continent's transformation. While the challenges are real, the dominant spirit of Africans is hope fueled by energy and determination to bring about a better life for themselves and their children. The following chapter will explore how foundations and corporate grantmakers developed their initial strategies for working in Africa.

CHAPTER 4

Developing a Strategy for Grantmaking in Africa

"The hard part of grinding is the first grinding; when that is done the rest is easy." (Hausa proverb from Nigeria and Niger)

Link Mission and Strengths to Africa ⋏ Conduct Research ⋏ Engage Consultants
⋏ Network ⋏ Make Site Visits ⋏ Keep an Open Mind ⋏ Be Focused

The first steps toward making grants in Africa can be daunting. It is easy to feel overwhelmed by the vastness of the continent and the magnitude of need. The danger, as Ed Ahnert of ExxonMobil suggests, is that "American grantmakers want to remake the world in their image rather than help people become what they want to become themselves. We tend to take our own belief systems and inflate them to become universal truths. These truths may not be so universally held in other societies." Following are some practical suggestions for getting started based on interviews with grantmakers already engaged in Africa.

Link Mission and Strengths to Africa

When asked how they started their programs in Africa, nearly all longtime grantmakers responded that the starting point was their foundation's original mission and grantmaking focus in the United States. They saw their funding in Africa as a natural extension of their foundation's domestic programs, whether they focus on health, education, population, civil society, the environment or other areas. Newer foundations, on the other hand, are more likely to start with a founder's passion for a particular issue, such as children or HIV/AIDS, and then discover that Africa offers excellent opportunities for making an impact.

In both cases, the key is to begin with the foundation's mission and core values. As Nancy Muirhead of the Rockefeller Brothers Fund puts it, "Do your homework, discover your area of expertise, look for where that resonates in Africa, start from what you know and start from your strengths."

The W.K. Kellogg Foundation of Battle Creek, Michigan, for example, has made grants to disadvantaged groups and community self-help projects in Michigan and throughout the United States since 1930. In the late 1980s, the foundation embarked on a grantmaking program in South Africa in direct response to the human rights abuses of that country's apartheid regime. It began by funding scholarships to enable disadvantaged South Africans to obtain undergraduate degrees in South Africa and advanced degrees from universities outside the country. Kellogg also made grants in South Africa to community-based organizations and universities for health, education and rural development projects. From these initial first steps, the Kellogg Foundation expanded its current Southern Africa regional program to include education and leadership support as well as integrated rural development. Today, Kellogg maintains a regional office in Pretoria, the capital of South Africa, staffed by 16 Africans, and its program budget is currently about $20 million a year, representing 8 percent of the foundation's total grantmaking.

Another example is the Trinity Church Grants Program in New York City, established in the 1970s to support the mission and ministry of the Anglican Church and other ecumenical organizations. Trinity decided to focus its giving on Africa because the Anglican Church was growing rapidly there and the needs were great. To develop its strategy, Trinity Church created an International Advisory Council on Telecommunications for the Anglican Community. Based on the council's conclusion in 2000 that improved telecommunications capacity was critical to carry out the mission and ministry of the church, the Trinity Church Grants Program took up the challenge.

Trinity's annual grantmaking budget of $1.2 million goes to two programs areas: strengthening telecommunications in the Anglican community and strengthening the church in the global South, both primarily focused on Africa. In Nigeria, one of Trinity's grants supported a week-long technology-training program for 152 leaders of the Nigerian Anglican Church. It later helped establish the first global private network of the Anglican community in the southern hemisphere using satellite communication. The Anglican churches in Kenya and Tanzania are now fully "wired." In Africa, the Trinity Church Grants Program also funds projects on HIV/AIDS, community development, distance learning, primary and preventive healthcare and leadership training.

The Global Catalyst Foundation, established in 2000 in Redwood Shores, California, provides another example of linking core mission to opportunities in Africa. The foundation was created by the principals of Global Catalyst Partners, a Silicon Valley venture capital firm with a mission to improve people's lives through the effective application of information technologies. The foundation initiates and supports small-scale, innovative projects around the world that harness information and communication technologies to empower communities. The Global Catalyst Foundation embarked on grant-making in Africa after the chairman visited the Mtabila refugee camp near the town of Kasulu in western Tanzania. The camp's 45,000 refugees from conflict in neighboring Burundi lacked access to educational opportunities for building skills that could lead to employment. Using a small vocational college's computer school in Kasulu, Global Catalyst teamed up with the United Nations Development Programme, the United Nations High Commissioner for Refugees (UNHCR), Schools Online, and the Tanzania Commission on Science and Technology, as well as a Kasulu Internet Steering Committee and a Mtabila camp Internet committee to develop a program to bring computers, Internet access and skills training to the residents of the camp.

Conduct Research

There is really no substitute for thoughtful research on the issues and countries that look like they might fit with a foundation's mission and values. A lot of information already exists — on the Internet, in libraries, with multilateral organizations like the World Bank and UNDP, and with operational NGOs working in specific countries or sectors in Africa. The Foundation Center's database tracks all grants of $10,000 or more made by U.S. grantmakers and can be searched for grants of various kinds to African countries. A list of selected resources for conducting research on Africa can be found in Appendix I.

In addition, other foundations already working in the same areas may be willing to help by sharing their research and suggesting gaps in their own programs. In 1998, when California's Packard Foundation first began to develop a country strategy for a population program in Nigeria, the program officer contacted The MacArthur Foundation, which had an office in that country and a 10-year grantmaking track record in the population area. MacArthur's program staff, at both MacArthur's headquarters in Chicago and in Nigeria, helped Packard to identify needs that were under-funded, arranged meetings with other funders and potential grantee partners, and served as a sounding board to refine Packard's initial strategic directions. The collaboration between the two foundations continues to this day.

It may also be useful to research the development policies and priorities of the specific countries in which you have a funding interest. While it may not always be feasible or appropriate, linking your foundation or corporation's grantmaking to a wider national strategy or action plan could increase the impact of your funding. That has been the experience of the Packard Foundation whose population program in Nigeria supports the Nigerian Government's policy of slowing population growth by extending access to family planning and related reproductive health services to underserved populations, especially in the northern region of the country.

Engage Consultants With Care

External consultants can be useful in gathering information, developing a coherent strategy and identifying options for funders. Seasoned grantmakers, however, urge caution. Not all consultants, even if they have traveled or worked in Africa, have the right kind of knowledge or experience. Kakuna Kerina of the Open Society Initiative for West Africa laments that "Africa is the only continent where there are so many overnight experts impacting significantly on Africa policy and the allocation of limited external resources." It is wise to research potential consultants and check their references to make sure they have extensive experience with grantmaking in Africa before engaging them.

The Minneapolis-based McKnight Foundation, established in 1953, is a family foundation that devotes more than 80 percent of its grants budget and most of its energy to efforts in Minnesota. The foundation has a strong commitment to improving the quality of life for present and future generations as well as seeking paths to a more humane and secure world. After deciding to target some of its resources toward the needs of women in Africa, McKnight hired an experienced consultant to organize a three-week visit for staff and board members to Zimbabwe, Tanzania and Uganda. After learning first-hand about the economic challenges facing African women from grassroots and women's advocacy groups, as well as from business leaders and public officials in the three countries, the McKnight Foundation developed an initial Africa program strategy focusing on small grants to projects in the three countries that support women's economic and social empowerment.

The Izumi Foundation of Boston, Massachusetts, was created in 1999 to enhance the goals of Shinnyo-En USA, a lay Buddhist organization. Before embarking on a program to reduce infectious diseases in Africa, Izumi contacted a consulting firm that could research and develop a strategic approach and grantmaking guidelines for the foundation. Izumi admits that the consultants were not as familiar with Africa as they needed to be. As a result, the foundation encountered difficulty aligning a very broad mission with available program resources.

Many foundations point out the availability of highly trained and experienced Africans who have been instrumental in helping them shape their Africa program strategies. These talented professionals exist in every country working with NGOs, governments, universities, multilateral organizations and the private sector. Referrals from NGOs and foundations already working in a particular country can provide good leads. Contacting NGOs, universities and government agencies directly can also lead to the right person for a consultancy. These African consultants are already on site and can save on consultant travel costs. More importantly, they speak the relevant languages, understand the local context and culture, and provide access to extensive in-country networks and resources, all of which can be invaluable to a foundation seeking to find an appropriate and realistic funding niche.

Network

Most new grantmakers in Africa find that networking with other funders already active on the continent and interested in the same issue areas is vital in formulating their program. But how do you find other funders? Grantmaking affinity groups are one good source. The principal resource is the Africa Grantmakers' Affinity Group (AGAG), which includes more than 35 foundations of all types and sizes sharing a common interest in Africa. AGAG convenes an annual meeting, holds briefings on initiatives of interest to Africa grantmakers, and maintains an e-mail list server of foundations and corporations active in Africa. Funders Concerned About AIDS (FCAA) has an international programmatic focus on HIV/AIDS rather than a specific geographic focus on Africa, although many of FCAA's 2,000 constituent members make grants in Africa. Another affinity group with international interests that include Africa is Grantmakers Without Borders, a subgroup of the National Network of Grantmakers, which promotes social change philanthropy around the world. By connecting with established interest groups, new grantmakers in Africa can test ideas, learn about effective practices, identify partners and move their strategic planning processes forward. A list of affinity groups interested in Africa is provided in Appendix I.

Another networking option is to participate in conferences, both in the United States and abroad, that include issues of special relevance to grantmakers in Africa. Conferences can be valuable for connecting with other grantmakers who are more experienced in Africa or who are working on similar issues. They are also cited as an important way of learning about current trends, finding out what other grantmakers are doing, and learning how they are addressing challenges.

The Firelight Foundation of Santa Cruz, California, was started in 1999 by Kerry Olson, an educator and advocate for children's rights. With an initial interest in the impact of HIV/AIDS on children in Africa in mind, she attended the U.N. Conference on Children Orphaned by AIDS in December of 1999. She also met with the director of the White House Office on National AIDS Policy and the Council on Foundations, confirming the urgent needs of children in communities impacted by this disease. From there, Firelight staff traveled to Africa, identified several grassroots groups and made some initial grants.

The Council on Foundations Annual Conference normally includes several sessions relevant to grantmaking in Africa and draws participants from African foundations. Grantmakers Without Borders holds an annual conference focused on grantmaking for social change in Africa and other developing regions. In addition, the Global Philanthropy Forum organized by the World Affairs Council of Northern California draws foundations, corporations and individual funders to its annual meetings, which include speakers and sessions on Africa. CIVICUS, the World Voluntary Organization for Citizen Participation, is headquartered in South Africa and holds a global forum at a different location around the world every two years.

Make Site Visits

Acknowledging that site visits may not be practical for some foundations, especially smaller foundations with few, if any, staff, most grantmakers interviewed underscored the importance of site visits in developing a foundation's strategy for Africa. At some point in their program development process, most funders carry out at least one visit to Africa during which they meet with international aid organizations and other funders as well as locally-based NGOs, experts and potential grantee groups. Through these discussions, grantmakers refine where and how they can make a difference with their resources and they may identify local advisors who can help guide the grantmaking program over time. In some cases, as part of the learning process, initial site visits can result in small, trial grants to groups with potential as longer-term partners. Site visits can also be useful at significant junctures in a funder's history as it reviews previous strategies with grantees and seeks their input on new grantmaking approaches.

Who should make site visits? Experience suggests a grantmaking strategy that has the strong backing of a foundation's board and senior management is more likely to be sustained and supported over the long term. Commitment to a program in Africa typically increases after a visit by senior management and trustees.

For example, on its 10th anniversary in 1997, The Global Fund for Women-based in San Francisco, California, noted that only 12 percent of its grants were going to women's groups in Africa, a figure that reflected neither the needs nor the strengths of African women's organizations. As part of a broad-based planning effort a group of 20 people, consisting of board members, staff and long-time supporters of the organization, visited eight countries in Africa in order to understand better the challenges facing African women, to seek feedback on the Fund's grantmaking approach, to meet local activists who could serve on the Fund's advisory council, and to increase the Fund's visibility among African women's groups. The group split up into teams that held forums hosted by local organizations. As a result of this listening-and-learning visit, The Global Fund for Women developed a plan to guide its funding in Africa. Since 1998, the Fund's grantmaking in Africa has more than tripled as has the number of advisory council members based in Africa.

The Clarence Foundation of Albany, California, was established in 1999 with the mission of helping innovative and successful grassroots organizations to grow to the next level. It identified five broad areas of interest: children, education, health, human rights and women. In January 2001, the foundation's executive director and a board member undertook a two-week fact-finding trip to the Democratic Republic of Congo. Upon returning, the Clarence Foundation created an Africa Philanthropy Circle of donors to review grant requests and refine areas of interest. The Africa Circle soon led to the development of a larger global giving initiative which enabled groups of donors to pool their time, talent and resources to support small projects in Africa and around the world. Clarence's first grant in Africa was to a microcredit program in Kinshasa that also helps people save for medical emergencies.

Keep an Open Mind

Throughout the process of exploring the possibilities of grantmaking in Africa and crafting an appropriate strategy, seasoned grantmakers consistently urge keeping an open mind. Nancy Muirhead with the Rockefeller Brothers Fund advises, "Consult as broadly as possible, listen attentively and don't come in with your own blueprint." In a continent as diverse as Africa, grantmakers can usually identify points of common interest for support and funding, but they should take care to find opportunities that fit local needs and conditions as well. Buttressing this view, Duncan Whiteside with the Maidstone Foundation counsels grantmakers, "Do not prescribe ideas; support people with their own ideas." That view is echoed by Gail McClure of the Kellogg Foundation, who urges grantmakers to be willing to learn from Africa, "Don't think of Africa as something broken that you are going to fix. Go with respect to find mutual ground. You will learn as much as you give." Cornelia Higginson with American Express points out that part of the experience of working in Africa is that "your assumptions will be challenged at every turn."

Be Focused

Based on the interviews for this book, there is no single route for a grantmaker to follow in developing a strategy for funding in Africa. Rather, this chapter has highlighted some of the essential elements for arriving at a funding strategy that makes sense for a particular grantmaker — thinking about mission, doing basic research, working with qualified consultants, networking and making site visits.

The advice from seasoned grantmakers that stands out most is the need to focus funding as much as possible. Is a formal strategic plan for Africa essential to achieve that focus? Not necessarily. About half the foundations interviewed have adopted some kind of formal strategy or program paper to guide their work in Africa. The plans look ahead for periods of three to 10 years and often harmonize a specific strategy for Africa with larger institutional goals. Other grantmakers simply apply their organization's established worldwide funding guidelines to Africa without developing a separate sub-strategy for the region.

However, even if there is no formal plan, it is prudent to go through at least an informal research and planning process that identifies the initial direction and parameters of the grantmaker's funding in Africa. This might include focusing on a region or country, and/or in a specific grantmaking sector, ideally tied to domestic grantmaking strengths. The alternative is likely to be a scattershot approach that leads to poor results and dissatisfaction for both grantmaker and grantees.

In determining the best approach, grantmakers should ask themselves several questions:

■ What are the issues that reflect our mission and values?

■ Where in Africa are needs around those issues especially acute?

■ What is the general environment for making grants in those countries or localities?

■ Where is success or the biggest impact likely to occur?

■ Which funders are working there already (to complement our activities) and where are the gaps that we could fill?

Of course, funding programs can and do change in response to factors that are both internal and external to the foundation, so initial funding strategies are only starting points. It is almost certain that the strategy will evolve over time with the accumulation of experience and deeper knowledge.

CHAPTER 5

Funding in Africa through U.S. and International Organizations

"The help you give others will soon be your own." (Ewe proverb from Ghana, Benin and Togo)

U.S. Nonprofit Private Voluntary Organizations U.S. Intermediary Organizations
U.S. Government Multilateral Organizations

O nce an approach, specific issue area(s) and a geographic focus for funding in Africa are narrowed, it is necessary to identify appropriate funding partners. The range of choices can be dizzying. Do you want to start off by funding a familiar U.S.-based nonprofit private voluntary organization that operates programs in Africa? Or, do you prefer to work with an African non-governmental organization or public agency directly? Or, perhaps an organization based in Canada or Europe that does good work in Africa, or maybe a multilateral organization like the U.N. Development Programme or UNICEF with significant programs throughout the continent? There are pros and cons to each of these options, and grantmakers must assess them in light of their own unique missions, objectives, values and resources.

U.S. Nonprofit Private Voluntary Organizations

It is not necessary to give a grant to an organization in Africa in order to fund a program there. Dozens of U.S.-based 501(c)(3) nonprofit organizations, also called private voluntary organizations (PVOs), operate programs throughout Africa. These operational organizations are sustained by contributions from the American public, foundations, corporations and government. Well-known examples include U.S.-based international relief and development organizations like Africare, The Africa-America Institute, CARE, Oxfam America, Catholic

Relief Services and World Vision International. But many smaller and less well-known American PVOs are also engaged in Africa as well. Large and small, religious or secular, they encompass a wide spectrum of programs ranging from eliminating river blindness (Helen Keller Worldwide) to financing microenterprise (The Trickle Up Program) to supporting children and community development (Save the Children). A good source of information on U.S. PVOs working in Africa is the American Council for Voluntary International Action (InterAction) in Washington, D.C. InterAction is a national umbrella organization for U.S. private voluntary organizations working internationally and more than 100 of its 160 members have projects or programs in Africa. See the resources section in Appendix I for contact information.

The advantages of funding through an established U.S. 501(c)(3) PVO that has public charity status include the comfort level that comes with funding a known entity with a proven track record, professional management and staff, access to operational programs on the ground in Africa, and — not least — U.S. 501(c)(3) tax-deductible charitable status. Having charitable status with the Internal Revenue Service means that a foundation can make a grant to the organization with administrative ease. In addition, these organizations have the capacity to handle both large and small grants and they typically have strong accounting and reporting systems in place to meet donors' requirements.

For all of these reasons, smaller grantmakers just getting starting funding in Africa often choose to work through established PVOs with 501(c)(3) status. As Catherine Bryant of the Izumi Foundation notes, "If you are a small foundation, funding internationally can be a very daunting task." Even larger, more experienced grantmakers choose to work through established U.S. PVOs. The McKnight Foundation made a grant to Atlanta-based CARE for a program in Tanzania to assist women to develop environmentally friendly small businesses on the island of Zanzibar. American Express gave $300,000 as part of a ten-year commitment to the World Monuments Fund in New York to save endangered heritage sites throughout Africa.

On the other hand, operational PVOs are ordinarily looking for support for their own ongoing program activities. If a foundation wants to give a grant to the organization to do something additional or an activity that is outside the existing program framework of the PVO, the foundation may find the organization lacks the expertise it desires or the PVO may decline the grant offer. Obviously, the larger the potential grant, the more leverage a foundation or corporation may have to shape the programs of an operational PVO.

Another consideration is the degree of contact with beneficiaries in Africa that a grantmaker desires. Making grants through U.S. PVOs puts an organizational middleman between the grantmaker and the ultimate beneficiaries of the grant. In fact, the U.S. PVO may re-grant the funds to yet another organization, perhaps a local African non-governmental organization, to carry out the project activities, so there may be several intermediaries between the grantmaker and ultimate recipients. Donor briefings and tours can help to bridge the distance, but if the grantmaker's goal is to have a close, ongoing relationship with the beneficiaries of its Africa grants, funding through a U.S. PVO may not be the best choice.

Valentine Doyle of the Lawson Valentine Foundation represents the perspective of a small family foundation that started funding programs in Africa in 1992. "You can dive in as deep as you want," Doyle points out, "but there are easy ways to start — at the shallow end. Find a U.S. program you really trust and work with them. We've funded several village projects in West Africa through World Neighbors, a wonderful group. Sure, it would be more exciting to be up close and personal, but chances are that an organization with staff on the ground will do a better job."

U.S. Intermediary Organizations

In response to the rapid rise of grantmaker interest in international funding opportunities over the past decade, a number of U.S.-based public charities now offer special fee-based services in addition to their own grantmaking activities. These services are designed to meet the needs of U.S. foundations and corporations that wish to give outside the United States but prefer not to take on the responsibilities of doing so directly. Unlike the American PVOs discussed earlier, which mostly implement their own programs, these intermediary organizations are re-granters. Their services vary by organization but may include setting up a donor-advised fund, identifying an appropriate grantee organization, performing due diligence on the prospective grantee, transferring the funds, monitoring the grant, obtaining reports for the donor, and complying with legal requirements, both in the U.S. and in the grantee's country.

Some examples of this type of intermediary organization with expertise in Africa are Charities Aid Foundation America, The Global Fund for Women, the International Youth Foundation, the Tides Foundation, the Family Care Foundation and other public charities. (A longer list of intermediary organizations is provided on the Council on Foundations U.S. International Grantmaking website at www.usig.org.) These foundations all have staff or networks of advisors and partners in Africa to assist them in fulfilling their role as intermediaries. Therefore, a foundation or corporation that wishes to make a grant for a particular purpose but is not aware of potential local African grantee organizations can channel the grant through an intermediary organization that will identify an appropriate recipient. Or, a grantmaker that wishes to fund in a specific country but has no experience there can enlist the services of an intermediary organization to identify the best funding options. In general, a grantmaker may wish to consider funding through an intermediary organization if it does not have the knowledge, experience, administrative procedures and internal capacity to make the grants directly.

Many new grantmakers choose to fund through intermediaries to help them "test the international waters." Chris Allan of the Global Greengrants Fund urges grantmakers to "put your toe in the water; if that means working with an intermediary, do it." Larry Corley of the Family Care Foundation suggests that "for the smaller funder, it's very important to have a good intermediary organization." At the same time, Carol Berde of The McKnight Foundation cautions, "When you work with an intermediary, make sure their mission is completely congruent with yours."

An additional reason to fund through intermediaries is uncertainty about U.S. regulations for making direct overseas grants. These rules are currently under review by the Treasury Department and the Internal Revenue Service in the wake of 9/11 and the subsequent enactment of the USA PATRIOT Act and other counter-terrorism legal requirements. Consequently, some private foundations and corporations may feel uncertain about their legal obligations and how the rules may be interpreted or changed in the future. For them, funding internationally through a public charity intermediary may be a good option.

Citigroup Foundation does much of its international grantmaking through intermediary "friends of" organizations. For instance, in 2001 the Citigroup Foundation made a $50,000 grant to Charities Aid Foundation America (CAF America) for program development of a Moroccan NGO called Al-Amana. That same year, the Citigroup Foundation donated $30,000 through CAF America to support program development of an Algerian organization called Agence de Développment Social.

U.S. Government

The U.S. Agency for International Development (USAID) has primary responsibility for implementing the federal government's foreign aid programs. While at one time most U.S. foreign aid programs were implemented directly by USAID staff, that is no longer the case. The bulk of foreign aid funding is today channeled through private consulting firms, businesses, and nonprofit international relief and development NGOs for purposes ranging from agricultural development and healthcare to democracy-building and emergency assistance.

USAID's Global Development Alliance, undertaken in 2001, is an initiative to increase the agency's collaboration with both foundations and the private sector. The Bill & Melinda Gates Foundation, for instance, is the major contributor to the USAID/UNICEF Global Alliance for Vaccines and Immunization (GAVI) which is also supported by the Rockefeller Foundation and others. Another example is the Conrad N. Hilton Foundation's partnership with USAID on its Water for the Poor Alliance. The Hilton Foundation committed nearly $18 million in 2002 to provide clean drinking water to rural West African villages in Ghana, Mali and Niger as part of a broader public-private partnership with USAID and other non-governmental organizations.

Multilateral Organizations

Another option is to fund through a multilateral organization that has programs in Africa. The United Nations Development Programme (UNDP), the World Health Organization (WHO), the Food and Agriculture Organization (FAO) and the World Bank have all expressed interest in exploring how they can work more collaboratively with foundations and corporations. An advantage to working with multilateral organizations is that they often have staff and infrastructure on the ground in African countries. On the downside, however, multilateral institutions can be exceedingly bureaucratic and lack the flexibility or risk-taking spirit of foundations.

Nevertheless, multilateral organizations have achieved some effective partnerships with foundations. For example, Coca-Cola, reputedly Africa's largest employer, is working with the Joint United Nations Programme on HIV/AIDS (UNAIDS) in support of AIDS education and prevention efforts throughout the continent. Similarly, ExxonMobil provides grant funds to the Harvard Malaria Initiative, which works with the World Health Organization and the governments of five African countries to control this disease. The Ford Foundation and Charles Stewart Mott Foundation are jointly funding a community foundation initiative with the World Bank that may lead to integration of the community foundation concept into the bank's poverty reduction programs and replication of the model in Africa and elsewhere.

Smaller foundations in particular may wish to consider contributing to a specialized U.N. program such as UNICEF or working with the U.N.'s Fund for International Partnerships (UNFIP) to identify another appropriate U.N. agency. Contact information is listed in the resources section in Appendix I. Because specially designated international organizations like the U.N. and the World Bank are treated as public charities under IRS grantmaking rules, grants by U.S. private foundations and public charities to these organizations are relatively easy to make, provided that the funds are given for specific charitable purposes.

An alternative for foundations and corporations wishing to support the United Nations is to make a grant to the United Nations Foundation, based in Washington, D.C. The U.N. Foundation was established as a public charity in 1998 with a $1 billion commitment by Ted Turner to support the U.N. and augment the activities of its various specialized agencies. The foundation supports programs in 32 African countries.

CHAPTER 6

Options for Funding African Organizations

"Walking on another's property means being mild." (Lamba proverb from the Democratic Republic of Congo and Zambia)

African Community-Based Organizations ∿ African Non-Governmental Organizations
∿ African Grantmaking Foundations and Associations
∿ African Governments and Public Agencies

While the roots of Africa's modern civil society sector can be traced to the engagement of trade unions, women's movements and civic associations in the struggle against colonialism in the 1940s through the 1970s, the growth of the civil society sector has been most dramatic since the late 1980s. Today, the civil society sector in Africa is significant. According to the Comparative Nonprofit Sector Project of the Johns Hopkins Center for Civil Society Studies, 2.9 percent of adults in Uganda work in the nonprofit sector (including paid staff and volunteers). The figures are nearly as high for South Africa (2.5 percent), Tanzania (2.4 percent) and Kenya (2.3 percent). These figures are higher than in countries with more developed economies such as South Korea (1.9 percent), Brazil (1.4 percent) and Mexico (0.3 percent).

African Community-Based Organizations

Much like civil society organizations in the United States, indigenous African organizations encompass a wide and diverse field. The largest group consists of community-based organizations (CBOs) such as village committees, women's associations, neighborhood groups, agricultural cooperatives and youth sports leagues that have existed informally and without official recognition for generations.

They are closest to the ground and are therefore most capable of identifying and addressing local concerns. CBOs are also well positioned to prioritize local needs, mobilize communities for action, and navigate the often complex local cultural and political context. They rely heavily on traditional African values of volunteerism, cooperation, community spirit and resource sharing. African communities know that they must provide for their own needs rather than wait for government services. When formal governments are weak or absent as in Somalia, these community structures maintain social order and continuity at the local level. When governments are oppressive, CBOs can serve as engines of resistance as in South Africa under the apartheid regime or in Ethiopia under the Marxist Mengistu regime.

> *"In Africa where I come from there are thousands — if not millions — of informal groups of active citizens. Together they form social movements. They may not be visible to you, but they are to us, and we understand how crucial these informal networks have been to our survival. From this base, we are building more formal organizations, national umbrellas, and regional as well as pan-African networks, the kinds of organizations with which you are most likely to interact. If you trust us, we will open the way for you to come to know better all those millions of informal networks which exist and which have much to offer grantmakers."*
>
> — *Graça Machel, founder and chair of the Mozambique Foundation for Community Development, address at the European Foundation Centre Annual General Assembly, Lisbon, June 2003*

Funding African CBOs for specific project activities can be very rewarding for grantmakers, but funding them directly may also pose certain legal and logistical challenges for U.S. grantmakers. Most CBOs have no legal identity, they may not have a bank account or audit, and they may not be accessible by telephone or e-mail. In order to work with them, it may be advisable to fund through a U.S. NGO, an intermediary foundation, or an African NGO or foundation with strong grassroots linkages and local staff that can provide the required access and administrative support. The David and Lucile Packard Foundation, for instance, funds reproductive health programs with peasant associations in Ethiopia through two Ethiopian NGOs, the Amhara Development Association and the Oromo Development Association.

As the Global Greengrants Fund's Chris Allan points outs, "The great advances we now take for granted in the U.S. all started as grassroots movements. The grassroots is where durable change begins."

African Non-Governmental Organizations

Compared to CBOs, African non-governmental organizations (NGOs) tend to have a more formal structure, broader scope and, often, official status with their governments. There are African NGOs with programs in every field and they can be powerful forces for human progress. Some are small with a particular focus on, for instance, women's health, while others manage larger multi-faceted community development programs. Funders can sometimes maximize the impact of their grants by coordinating with other donors to support a single African NGO that is implementing several mutually reinforcing programs.

Examples of African NGOs include the Inter-Africa Group in Ethiopia with a focus on conflict resolution, the Institute for Adult Education in Tanzania, FEMNET (The African Women's Development and Community Network) based in Kenya, the Mozambican National Association for Rural Women Development, the Committee for Environmental Management in Togo, the Zimbabwe Women's Resource Center and Network plus thousands more. These organizations attract some of the most talented and visionary leaders in their countries, many of whom have worldwide stature. Duncan Whiteside of the Maidstone Foundation recommends that grantmakers "find the magnet person, the credible leader, and work alongside that person who has it right." Wangari Maathai, the founder of Kenya's Greenbelt Movement (a tree-planting organization) received the Goldman Environmental Prize awarded by the Richard and Rhoda Goldman Foundation of San Francisco in 1991. Daniel Robbins of the J.F. Kapnek Charitable Trust encourages grantmakers to "take the time to find the local talent and look for ways to support them."

In 2001, as a way of expanding its support for African NGOs, The Ford Foundation established the Special Initiative for Africa dedicated to seeking regional African solutions to three challenges: peace and conflict, citizenship and identity, and economic integration. Working with 50 African partner organizations and institutions like Liberia's Women in Peace-Building Network and South Africa's SaferAfrica, the Special Initiative has convened academics, activists and public officials from 30 countries to address these issues. In addition, the Special Initiative documents and disseminates information about successful African approaches to controlling small arms, negotiating conflict resolution, removing immigration barriers and fostering regional trade.

Despite the impressive achievements of many African NGOs, they tend to suffer from significant handicaps. They typically operate on shoestring budgets, usually dependent on external sources of funding, and often lack organizational capacity to fulfill their mission. Sometimes they lack basic equipment, such as computers and vehicles. Foundations and other donors may support program activities of African NGOs, but funds for basic operations, equipment, rent and salaries are often not forthcoming. Beyond these basics, funds for organizational planning, training, networking and advocacy are in short supply. Typical of the plea from African NGOs is one from Boge Gebre, Founder and President of the Kembatta Women's Self-Help Group in Ethiopia, who urges foundations to "fund programs, not projects; fund salaries and equipment."

Given the rapid proliferation of African NGOs in the past decade or so, a few words of caution are in order. Because many African NGOs are born of the energy and vision of a single charismatic individual, managing rapid organizational growth and transitioning to new leadership can be challenging. Moreover, the lure of international development aid for non-governmental organizations — from foreign governments, multilateral institutions, foundations and corporations — has triggered the emergence of opportunistic NGOs lacking a clear mission or popular base.

Seasoned grantmakers in Africa recommend carefully selecting African NGOs to partner with to ensure that there is a good match of interests, engaging with them for the long-term, and giving support for operational costs as well as to build the organization's capacity. Astrid Honeyman, formerly with the Bernard van Leer Foundation and now with Inter-Country People's Aid in Zimbabwe, urges grantmakers to "move beyond charity to capacity-building." Capacity-building, including professionalizing staff, establishing long-term strategies, diversifying fundraising, facilitating national and international networking, and engaging in advocacy, are viewed as an investment in the future of Africa's civil society. UNDP's Abdoulaye Ndiaye suggests that, "Every project should have a capacity-building element. Ultimately, it is the Africans who will develop themselves, not outside experts."

In an effort to connect with Africans, to ensure that projects are "locally-owned," and to build African NGO capacity, more and more U.S. grantmakers are choosing to work directly with African NGOs and grassroots groups. The Public Welfare Foundation in Washington, D.C., has been making grants in Africa for many years to combat HIV/AIDS and female genital mutilation. Initially, the foundation funded exclusively through international NGOs. However, in the early 1990s the foundation's board decided to transfer most of the grants to African NGOs like the Babiker Badri Scientific Association for Women's Studies in Sudan and the Coptic Organization for Services and Training in Egypt, believing that these organizations would have the best knowledge and understanding of how to address Public Welfare's issue areas. The possibilities of funding African NGOs with grants both large and small are unlimited.

African Grantmaking Foundations and Associations

Africa has deep traditions of personal and religious-based philanthropy. Traditional African cultures teach the obligation to share with one's extended family, neighbors and community in times of hardship. Today, while personal and religious-based philanthropy are still strong, indigenous philanthropy in Africa is becoming more secular and more institutional. Grantmaking foundations of many types exist in Africa and, while they are in many cases dependent on non-African foundations and corporations for much of their funding, they are also building a local donor base and represent a significant feature of Africa's dynamic civil society sector.

Since it was created in 1995, the Southern Africa Grantmakers Association (SAGA) has grown to more than 80 members, including corporations, family foundations, and community foundations, plus several American and European foundations. Foundations linked to well-known South African leaders like the Nelson Mandela Children's Fund and the Desmond Tutu Educational Trust are members of SAGA.

In East Africa a regional organization called *Ufadhili*, the Kiswahili word for philanthropy, was launched in 2002. Ufadhili operates the Centre for Philanthropy and Social Responsibility in Nairobi, Kenya and provides a support network for a growing number of corporate and family foundation grantmakers in Kenya, Uganda and Tanzania. A Ford Foundation grant enabled Ufadhili to become established so that it can build a network of technical support for philanthropy in the region. Another Ford grant to Allavida, a UK-based international development NGO, supported the emerging East Africa Association of Grantmakers that was ultimately launched in 2003. Ford has also made a series of capacity-building grants to individual East African foundations like the UZIMA Foundation in Nairobi, which focuses on youth behavior and leadership programs. UZIMA youth groups now number over 100 with a membership of nearly 20,000 young people. A grant to UZIMA from the Rockefeller Foundation in 2000 funded an assessment of the UZIMA Foundation's program impact.

While the indigenous grantmaking sector has been most advanced in the Southern Africa and East Africa regions, African foundations can also be found in other parts of the continent. The African Women's Development Fund (AWDF), for example, was formed in 2001 in Accra, Ghana but makes grants throughout the Sub-Saharan region. The Ford Foundation, Carnegie Corporation of New York, The Global Fund for Women and several other funders provided start-up grants to AWDF. With these funds, AWDF awarded grants ranging from $1,000 to $25,000 to more than 132 African women's organizations in 2001/2002, totaling more than $1 million. AWDF's Executive Director Bisi Adeleye-Fayemi feels that the organization's partnerships with U.S. foundations have been positive and mutually reinforcing. Multi-year commitments from American funders have been especially appreciated as well as the focus on building AWDF's capacity and providing pass-through funds for re-granting to local African women's organizations.

Adeleye-Fayemi also points out the value of non-financial support that U.S. foundations have given AWDF such as international networking opportunities to introduce the organization to new potential donors in the United States. At the same time, she notes that "learning is not a one-way street from the U.S. to Africa; American funders learn a lot about local conditions and realistic strategies from their African counterparts." Examples of other African foundations include the West African Rural Foundation in Senegal, the Obafemi Awolowo Foundation in Nigeria, the Mwalimu Nyerere Foundation in Tanzania, the Cameroon Gatsby Trust and the Africa Foundation in South Africa. The Sawiris Foundation in Egypt is one of the new, private foundations that are being established without external support. More African foundations exist and the number is growing.

Community foundations, combining African traditions of community action and helping one's neighbors with the American organizational concept, are being established in various parts of Africa, including South Africa, Mozambique, Zimbabwe and Kenya. Like community foundations in the United States, these organizations are run by boards of community leaders, and they make grants to community groups based on local priority needs. "Community foundations connect to a broad range of groups working for the common good," notes Inviolatta Moyo, Executive Director of the Community Foundation of the Western Region of Zimbabwe. As in the United States, community foundations can be powerful mechanisms for strengthening civic participation, funding civil society, and empowering communities to build a better future.

Several American foundations have been leaders in supporting the community foundation movement in Africa. The Charles Stewart Mott Foundation has made several large grants to the Greater Rustenberg Community Foundation and the Uthungulu Community Foundation in South Africa. The Mott, Ford and Kellogg foundations also jointly supported the Community Foundations Pilot Program at the Southern African Grantmakers Association (SAGA). In addition, The Ford Foundation provides financial and technical support to the Kenya Community Development Foundation (KCDF), which makes grants to strengthen community organizations in Kenya.

One way for U.S. grantmakers to fund community-based projects in areas served by African community foundations is to channel grants through them. In doing so, the community foundation's capacity, credibility and visibility in the community are all enhanced. The McKnight Foundation of Minnesota made a grant to the Synergos Institute to support the Community Foundation of Western Zimbabwe, which makes grants for education, women's economic empowerment, youth development, water and HIV/AIDS to grassroots organizations and rural district councils in three provinces: Matabeleland South, Matabeleland North and Midland. Similarly, the Bernard van Leer Foundation, based in the Netherlands, used the Kenya Community Development Foundation as an intermediary to work with five grantees in Kenya that implement community-based early childhood development programs. Part of van Leer's grant stays with the KCDF to help the five grantees to strengthen their institutional capacity while the other part is re-granted to the five organizations to meet individual needs.

> **"In forging (sub)regional links and in setting up exclusively Southern networks, as well as in partnering with a democratic and co-operative state, civil society in Africa is well on its way to leaving the children's table of global politics and taking its deserved seat among the global players."**
>
> — *Kumi Naidoo, Secretary General, CIVICUS: World Alliance for Citizen Participation*

African Governments and Public Agencies

Just as foundations and corporations may make grants to public universities, libraries, museums, research centers and other public bodies in the U.S., there are many opportunities to do so in sub-Saharan Africa. In fact, under IRS rules, grants by U.S. private foundations and public charities to units of foreign governments or public agencies abroad are relatively easy to make since they are exempt from more rigorous procedures required of private recipient organizations.

For example, the Bill & Melinda Gates Foundation, Merck & Co., and the Merck Company Foundation are collaborating with others on a major HIV/AIDS initiative with the Government of Botswana. "This is a project driven by the Republic of Botswana. We are not coming in with solutions," points out Linda Distlerath, Merck's vice president of global health policy. "We can offer resources and expertise that might be useful," Distlerath continues, "but this is really based around the Republic of Botswana and its National Strategic Framework for HIV/AIDS. They identify where our resources can be put to the best use."

In 2000, the Rockefeller Foundation, the John D. and Catherine T. MacArthur Foundation, Carnegie Corporation of New York and The Ford Foundation launched a $100 million joint initiative now called the Partnership for Higher Education in Africa. Makerere University in Uganda, the University of Dar es Salaam in Tanzania, Eduardo Mondlane University in Mozambique, plus a number of universities in Ghana and Nigeria are among the higher education institutions that are being assisted through this program. The collaboration enables the funders to coordinate their resources, achieve administrative efficiencies, and share what they learn. Each foundation is continuing to support universities in particular countries where it has longstanding ties to the higher education community.

The Kresge Foundation has supported construction and renovation projects at the University of Cape Town and the University of Pretoria in South Africa by using challenge grants to bring in other corporate, foundation and individual donors. The American University in Cairo is supported by grants from several major U.S. foundations including Ford, Rockefeller, Hewlett and Mellon as well as corporate foundations like Citigroup, General Electric and BP Amoco. The Carnegie Corporation of New York, in addition to its support for African universities, makes grants to revitalize public libraries in South Africa, Botswana and Kenya, much as its founder Andrew Carnegie did in the United States and elsewhere a century ago.

Individuals

Not all foundations make grants to individuals. But some do, generally for research, education, training or leadership development. In Nigeria, for example, The MacArthur Foundation set up a Fund for Leadership Development to make grants to mid-career professionals working in the population and reproductive health field. The Rockefeller Foundation has a long history of making individual grant awards each year to individuals for postdoctoral research in health, agriculture and other development-related fields primarily at African universities.

Similarly, The Ford Foundation's $280 million 10-year International Fellowships Program launched in 2000 marks a significant expansion of Ford's previous support for advanced educational opportunities for exceptional individuals from Africa and other developing regions. The Ford Foundation implements the program in Africa through several private voluntary organizations: the Association of African Universities (for Ghana, Nigeria and Senegal), the Africa-America Institute (for Mozambique and South Africa) and America-Mideast Educational and Training Service (for Egypt). Likewise, the Kellogg Foundation supports individual scholarships for undergraduate and graduate education for Africans indirectly through American PVOs like the International Institute for Education and the Academy for Educational Development, which administer the scholarship programs.

This chapter and the preceding one have identified a range of funding options for grantmakers who are interested in becoming engaged in Africa. Some are easier administratively than others, while some may result in a richer experience but require more effort. The right option depends on a variety of individual grantmaker factors, including grant size, internal management capacity, grantmaking philosophy and program focus. The advice from experienced grantmakers is not to be overwhelmed by all the choices. "Don't wait for the perfect collaboration or the perfect needs assessment," urges Family Health International's Suzi Peel, a former Firelight Foundation advisory board member, "do something now."

CHAPTER 7

Working Effectively with African Grantees

"The one who listens is the one who understands." (Jabo proverb from Liberia)

Publicizing Grant Criteria and Soliciting Proposals ⁄⌃ Conducting Due Diligence
⁄⌃ Complying with Legal Requirements ⁄⌃ Transferring Funds to Africa ⁄⌃
Monitoring Grants ⁄⌃ Managing Grants — Staffing Models

Whether making a small or large grant, funding at the community or national levels, or working in any sector, experienced grantmakers in Africa agree that the key to effective grantmaking is the relationship with the grantee. Fundamentally, it is not about money but about partnership. As Cornelia Higginson of The American Express Philanthropic Program puts it, "If you have the attitude we are giving them $1 million so they better do what we say, you can't expect results long-term. You must really involve people in a process, in an exploration. Money is the least of it." Randall Cooper of the Cogitare Foundation offers similar advice: "Don't just dole out money, get involved personally."

At the same time, grantmakers in Africa acknowledge that smoothing out the unequal power dynamics inherent in a grantor-grantee relationship to arrive at one that is more trustful, collegial and collaborative takes time as well as a high degree of personal engagement on the part of both donor and grantee. But it is well worth the effort. In developing a positive relationship with grantees, experienced grantmakers in Africa advise slowing down, having patience, establishing trust through an ongoing personal connection, and showing respect for the grantee's traditions, values and experience. In building effective partnerships with African grantees, it is also important for grantmakers to acknowledge that they do not come with the answers, that they make mistakes and that they want to learn from and alongside the grantee. The Commonwealth Secretariat's Adaora Ikenze, drawing on her previous experience with the Global Fund for Women, advises: "Don't come with an agenda. Let your agency be as open and as flexible as possible."

In addition to openness and flexibility, grantmakers are encouraged to adjust their time horizon for working in Africa. "Think long term," urges Don Mohanlal of the International Youth Foundation, which has funded in Africa since 1992, "and don't get discouraged from the first mistakes." Missteps are inevitable, especially for grantmakers new to Africa, and seasoned grantmakers understand that making mistakes is part of the learning process. In addition to allowing time for satisfying partnerships to evolve, long-term relationships with appropriate African organizations are more likely to contribute to solving Africa's problems, most of which are not subject to short-term solutions. "If you can think in terms of 15 or 20 years, you may be on the mark. You can do many projects, but you can only change things in that period," notes Duncan Whiteside of the Maidstone Foundation.

Daniel Robbins of the J.F. Kapnek Charitable Trust, which funds exclusively in politically troubled Zimbabwe, encourages grantmakers to "be patient and stay the course; don't leave when the going gets tough politically; it engenders distrust and dislike." Inviolatta Moyo, executive director of the Community Foundation for the Western Region of Zimbabwe, reflects the African perspective when she notes that when a foundation suspends funding or shifts areas of funding emphasis it is highly disruptive and undermines the relationship between grantor and grantee.

These suggestions and many others for working effectively with African grantees are included in a document called the Guidelines for Good Practice for Northern Non-Governmental Organizations Working in South Africa adopted by the Southern African Grantmakers Association (SAGA) and the South African National NGO Coalition in 1998. The guidelines can be accessed through SAGA's website which is listed in the resources section in Appendix I.

Publicizing Grant Criteria and Soliciting Proposals

Some grantmakers to Africa do not accept unsolicited proposals, preferring instead a more proactive approach to identifying appropriate funding opportunities. For those that do accept unsolicited proposals, most use the Internet to publicize their mission, program focus, grant criteria, application process, deadlines and other requirements. When reaching out to organizations in Africa, it may be useful to specify whether proposals need to be in English and whether they must be typewritten.

Depending on which countries or region of Africa a grantmaker is targeting, it may also be useful to make the grantmaker's Web information available in French, Portuguese, Swahili or Arabic. If the grants program focuses on a specific country or region, providing information in one or more indigenous language may also be advisable. While publicizing grant programs in languages other than English requires that the grantmaking foundation or corporation have the necessary language skills available (either on staff or through consultants or advisors), the clear advantage is that the grantmaker is accessible to a wider range of Africans and funding opportunities are thereby expanded.

Bear in mind that small grassroots organizations in Africa may not have access to the Internet, especially in rural areas. Experienced grantmakers suggest going beyond the Internet to publicize grants programs and guidelines through more informal word-of-mouth channels involving in-country consultants, local advisors, NGOs active in the country or region of interest and other funders. Africa-based consultants and advisors as well as visiting U.S.-based foundation staff can also hold informational meetings and proposal-development workshops with potential grantees. Several grantmakers noted that some of their best grants evolved out of the interactions at these meetings.

Conducting Due Diligence

Conducting due diligence is a prerequisite for making grants directly to organizations in Africa or elsewhere in the world and normally begins with a careful review of the prospective grantee's organizational documents. While experienced grantmakers in Africa employ a variety of means to establish the *bonafides* of potential grantees, site visits by staff, advisors or consultants were most frequently mentioned. Several funders indicated that they never make a direct international grant without first conducting a site visit.

Since a site visit by foundation or corporate staff to every potential grantee may not always be feasible, other options exist. The Global Greengrants Fund, for instance, relies on recommendations from a series of advisory boards, composed of former grantees, issue experts, NGO leaders, scientists, activists and journalists who are familiar with many local groups ready for small funding. The recommendations are backed up by application forms and a standard affidavit in five languages that are reviewed by one of the advisory boards according to agreed-upon funding strategies. The Rockefeller Brothers Fund consults with experts in the field and former grantees after receiving an application. The Packard Foundation takes a different approach, engaging a major accounting firm to conduct pre-grant inquiries and due diligence on all grants above $50,000 through the firm's local offices in Africa. In South Africa, the Kresge Foundation sponsors occasional group workshops for nonprofit organizations on how to prepare competitive proposals for its capital grants program. In addition, Kresge offers appointments or structured conference calls with prospective grantees in advance of a formal application.

New or smaller funders to Africa may not have the staff or financial resources to conduct full due diligence or to make a site visit. For them, funding through a U.S.-based NGO or intermediary funding organization is a good option since that organization assumes the responsibility for fulfilling the due diligence requirements.

The process of verifying the legitimacy and organizational capacity of potential grantees need not be intimidating. Is the organization what it represents itself to be? Does it have the organizational capacity to implement the grant? Does it have strong leadership, good accounting practices and a solid reputation locally? Some funders seek out new organizations that have not previously benefited from foundation support, so there may be no track record, in which case site visits or the recommendations of trusted advisors who know the organization or leader well become crucial. As Larry Corley of the Family Care Foundation sees it, "Qualifying partners isn't rocket science. We look for people already doing something; we focus on the leader. We ask for photographs and evidence of strong local support, as well as reviewing the data provided on the standard application. Think of it in terms of good people doing good things."

Complying with Legal Requirements

Because U.S. legal requirements for making international grants are not specific to Africa, they will not be discussed in this book. For further information on the legal obligations of private foundations, public charities and corporations when making international grants, see the Council on Foundations' United States International Grantmaking website (www.usig.org), a collaboration with the International Center for Not-for-Profit Law. Also helpful are the following Council publications: *Beyond Our Borders, A Guide to Making Grants Outside the United States*, 1999, by John A. Edie and Jane C. Nober and *Expenditure Responsibility Step by Step*, 2001, by John A. Edie. Both can be ordered through the publications section of the Council's website (www.cof.org).

Like U.S. grantmakers funding anywhere in the world, those funding in Africa must comply with counter-terrorism requirements imposed by the U.S. Government in the wake of 9/11. Executive Order 13224 prohibits the transfer of funds or other material support to persons and organizations designated by the U.S. Government on various lists as terrorists. The USA PATRIOT Act of 2001 sets potential criminal penalties for any financial transaction involving an individual or organization on these lists. The best compilation of lists can be found on the website of the Treasury Department's Office of Foreign Assets Control (listed in Appendix I). For more information about the post-9/11 legal requirements for international grantmaking, see the Council on Foundations' United States International Grantmaking (USIG) website and *Grantmaking in an Age of Terrorism: Some Thoughts About Compliance Strategies*, by Janne G. Gallagher, Vice President and General Counsel at the Council on Foundations. The article is part of the Council's Legal Dimensions of International Grantmaking Series and can be downloaded from the International Programs section of the Council's website. Information about vendors that are beginning to provide services to help manage the implementation of these requirements is also listed on the USIG website. Another helpful resource is the *Handbook on Counter-Terrorism Measures: What U.S. Nonprofits and Grantmakers Need to Know* developed by the Council on Foundations, Independent Sector, InterAction and the law firm of Day, Berry & Howard. It can also be down-loaded from the Council's website.

Aside from the U.S. legal rules that affect international grants, grantmakers should also pay attention to the legal environment for charities and other nonprofits in the countries where the grant is being made. Many African countries do not yet have laws relating to the nonprofit sector and charitable giving, but some do. Do foreign donors need to be registered with the government? Legal profiles of the nonprofit and charity laws in Kenya, Nigeria and South Africa, researched and written by in-country legal experts, are posted on the United States International Grantmaking (USIG) website. Country information on the site is updated regularly.

Finally, like any legal specialty, the laws and rules regarding grantmaking internationally are not always clear and often require specialized expertise. Sometimes the basic information does not address all relevant questions or concerns. At that point, it is useful to contact peer foundations already working in the country under consideration to discuss their experience and to ask for references for U.S. attorneys who specialize in international grantmaking.

Transferring Funds to Africa

Africa's 54 different national banking systems vary greatly. It is therefore essential to investigate the currency rules and foreign exchange regulations of the specific country where a grantee is located before transferring funds directly. For instance, in some countries it may be possible to establish a U.S. dollar account while in others U.S. dollar transfers will be converted to local currency at the prevailing exchange rate for deposit in a local currency account.

Banks with operations in Africa tend to be strongest in urban areas and weak or even nonexistent in some rural areas. In the case of established African NGO grantees, most U.S. grantmakers routinely transfer funds by wire to the bank account of the grantee organization. Or alternatively, they courier or deliver a check in person to the grantee for deposit locally. In cases where the grantee does not already have a bank account — more typical of rural community-based groups — the grantee may either establish a new account at the nearest bank, often some distance away, or they may be allowed to share the bank account of another organization.

In some instances, establishing a bank account may not be an option due to banking regulations that prohibit certain types of organizations from opening accounts if they are not officially registered with the government. In that case, an account may be opened in the name of an individual, although it is advisable to require the signatures of at least two officials of the grantee organization for withdrawals.

Fund transfers to Africa are governed by the official exchange rates set either by a government or by the currency market. In some cases, exchange rate fluctuations and currency devaluations can dramatically alter the local purchasing power of a grant calculated at a more favorable exchange rate. Grantmakers should be aware of these fluctuations and flexible in terms of adjusting grants to make sure that they cover the project costs should a significant exchange rate fluctuation occur. In addition, bank fees and other transaction costs can be steep; these should also be built into the grant amount.

An ongoing issue with banks in Africa is that they sometimes delay acknowledging receipt of wire transfers in order to earn maximum interest on the funds
before they are deposited in the recipient's account. Frequent inquiries on the
part of the recipient and/or formal bank traces initiated by the grantor usually
resolve the issue.

Monitoring Grants

The keys to monitoring grants in Africa, according to experienced Africa
grantmakers, are to have clear, shared goals with the grantee as well as an
ongoing relationship. Good monitoring begins before the grant is even made.
"Be very clear on concrete outcomes," advises Kevin Starr of the Mulago
Foundation, who continues, "if you have a close, ongoing relationship with
your grantee, you will be much more likely to know what is going on." His
advice is amplified by Andrea Gay of the United Nations Foundation: "You
have to have measurable outcomes, pay attention, and show an interest."

Written reports are useful but may be of limited value. In Africa, with its
strong oral tradition of communication, community-based organizations may
be unaccustomed to preparing written reports for donors. Smaller, grassroots
organizations in particular may find it challenging to produce a typewritten
report in English. Moreover, they may not understand fully what the foundation
or corporation seeks in the report, perhaps seeing it as an opportunity to express
gratitude for the donor's generosity. Grantees may feel that it is impolite to
report anything negative about the project, even if due to circumstances
completely beyond their control, or they may refrain from doing so for fear
that further funding will be jeopardized. These tendencies can be overcome
by building trust through good communication of expectations.

Beyond reports, grants can be monitored using local consultants. A more
expensive option is to engage a professional accounting firm with an in-country
office to verify the accounting of the grant expenditure. But, according to
experienced grantmakers in Africa, the best way to monitor grants is to visit
and talk with grantees face-to-face. "Site visits are very enriching," says Bill

Moses of the Kresge Foundation, "They provide insights into local issues and conditions that are difficult to discern thousands of miles away."

Managing Grants Programs in Africa — Staffing Models

Among the experienced grantmakers interviewed for this book, no single model for managing grants to Africa emerged. Instead, depending on the size and resources available to a particular foundation or corporation, a range of workable models was described.

A few of the mainly larger U.S. grantmakers have offices and staff in Africa, including the Rockefeller Foundation (Kenya and Zimbabwe), The Ford Foundation (Kenya, Egypt, South Africa and Nigeria), the W.K. Kellogg Foundation (South Africa), The MacArthur Foundation (Nigeria), the Charles Stewart Mott Foundation (South Africa) and the Packard Foundation (Ethiopia and Nigeria). The smaller J.F. Kapnek Charitable Trust has an office in Zimbabwe, the sole focus of its program. These offices are the principal liaisons with existing and prospective grantees for program support, technical assistance and capacity-building. Administrative and financial management functions may be split between the field offices and headquarters or handled mainly from the U.S. In some cases, country nationals head the Africa offices; for example, the W.K. Kellogg Foundation's office in South Africa is entirely staffed by Africans.

Since most grantmakers cannot afford the expense of establishing an office in Africa or have only a limited involvement on the continent, the work of identifying potential grantees, building partnerships, and monitoring and evaluating grant programs must be carried out from the foundation's headquarters in the United States. Typically, a vice-president or program officer is charged with responsibility for the grantmaker's Africa program and travels to the continent one or more times a year to meet with current and prospective grantees. Between visits, communication by e-mail, telephone or letter can keep the relationship warm and alert the grantmaker to significant project developments that occur between visits.

To ensure an even closer level of engagement with grantees, some U.S.-based grantmakers hire consultants — either U.S.-based or Africa-based — to maintain relationships with grantees. The Packard Foundation employs a full-time consultant for its population program based in Ethiopia and relies on a part-time local expert in Nigeria. Their roles include conducting due diligence on grantees, supporting headquarters' staff when traveling in the region and, in some cases, providing technical assistance to grantees in the areas of capacity-building, monitoring and evaluation and reporting. These consultants are highly valued resources for the foundation and participate in annual meetings at Packard's offices in California.

Because the McKnight Foundation's primary grantmaking focus is on Minnesota, with funding in Africa representing only 1.5 percent of its total grants budget, the foundation employs U.S.-based consultants to manage its grants program, which supports women's social and economic empowerment in Tanzania, Uganda and Zimbabwe. The consultants make three to four trips to Africa each year to identify grantees, recommend grants to McKnight's board, provide technical assistance, and conduct post-grant monitoring. To support the work of the consultants, McKnight hires "national assistants" in each of the three countries for limited periods of time to support the consultants.

An alternative to establishing offices in Africa or hiring consultants is to create a network of African advisors. The Global Fund for Women, for instance, relies on a 120-member international advisory council that is organized into regional advisory networks. The Africa network is composed of 30 Africans who serve a three-year term and are paid a small honorarium. The Global Fund for Women depends on this network to provide staff with detailed feedback and contextual perspective on the women's groups it supports. Advisors provide valued input and knowledge of specific women's groups, link the Global Fund with groups interested in applying for grants, and provide advice on strategic initiatives. Most of the advisors are former Global Fund for Women grantees and activists in the field of women's human rights.

CHAPTER 8

How Grantmakers Approach Five Major Challenges in Africa

"Smooth seas do not make skillful mariners."
(Swahili proverb from East Africa)

Identifying and Maintaining a Focus ⁀ **Understanding the African Context**
⁀ **Bridging Cultural Differences** ⁀ **Achieving Sustainability**
⁀ **Measuring Impact**

Identifying and Maintaining a Focus

Many funders find the mere thought of Africa daunting with its myriad cultures, countries, languages, political systems and compelling needs. "The challenge is to keep focused and hold fast to the criteria of the program when there are so many appeals," notes Gail McClure of the Kellogg Foundation.

The collective wisdom of experienced Africa grantmakers is not to feel over-whelmed. Their consistent advice is to start with the foundation or corporation's strengths or core mission and to look for ways of linking them to Africa. "Operationalizing the mission is the hard part," observes Catherine Bryant of the Izumi Foundation.

Finding a focus may mean expanding a current domestic funding priority to Africa. Virtually any issue or problem that a foundation or corporation funds in the United States can be found in Africa. Most experienced grantmakers cite geographic focus as essential, recommending targeting funding in a way that resources can have a positive impact. Andrea Gay of the United Nations Foundation laments that "You can't have any impact if you don't focus, and it is hard to focus given the size of the continent and the extent of the issues."

Some grantmakers start by funding in only one community, like the Cogitare Foundation, which began by supporting a single school in one province of Zambia. Building on that experience, Cogitare subsequently broadened its grantmaking geographically to include programs in Mozambique and South Africa with further expansion planned.

Nancy Muirhead points out the challenge for the Rockefeller Brothers Fund this way: "There are myriad of good options, how do we fit in? The most difficult challenge is narrowing the possibilities. When we decided to work in South Africa with HIV/AIDS, we had 25 initial program ideas."

ADVICE BOX:

■ Start by linking grantmaking in Africa to the foundation's or corporation's mission and U.S. program focus.

■ Talk to other grantmakers and operational organizations about their programs in Africa that relate to your mission or focus.

■ Consult the expertise that exists within Africa.

■ Select a country or countries where organizations are doing work you admire or where individuals have a vision that reflects your values.

■ Look for gaps in existing programs, underserved areas or innovative groups to fund.

■ Collaborate initially with funders with more experience in Africa.

■ Start small, learn and increase your grantmaking over time.

Understanding the African Context

Navigating Africa's complexities can be challenging. Gail McClure of the W.K. Kellogg Foundation looks at it this way: "As Americans, we can seldom understand other cultures and contexts as well as our own or capture the subtle aspects and nuances of relationships required for sustainable development. While we have a lot to offer, we are the guests and the outsiders in other countries, and we have found that it works better to walk with some humility in that role and to share the power, resources and decisionmaking rather than try to set and implement an agenda on our own."

Experienced grantmakers understand that the context in which their grants are made may determine whether or not their objectives are achieved. A complex interplay of political, economic, social, cultural, environmental and other factors shapes that context, including everything from local tribal relations and gender issues to informal economies, official corruption and World Bank structural adjustment policies. As a result, for American funding organizations, especially the vast majority that do not have Africa-based staff, understanding adequately that context from a distance can be a real challenge. The consistent advice from experienced grantmakers is to learn from Africans themselves as well as from other funders and organizations already working there.

Most grantmakers will never become "experts" on Africa, but it is vitally important that they become savvy about those factors directly and indirectly affecting the particular context in which their grantmaking occurs. At the same time, grantmakers engaged in Africa caution against feeling overwhelmed and paralyzed by imperfect information or understanding. The key is to get started. Understanding will grow.

- Research issues and learn about communities or issues of interest by talking to knowledgeable individuals and participating in relevant conferences.

- Consult widely with African staff, advisors or consultants with expertise in the geographic area, specific sector or (sub)culture in which grants will be made, bearing in mind that each country of Africa is unique and don't assume that experiences can be transferred automatically from one to another.

- Create a proposal review network or advisory committee composed of Africans with experience and knowledge relevant to your grantmaking focus.

- Consider funding initially through experienced intermediary organizations.

- Stay in touch with grantees through regular communication.

- Visit grantees as often as you can and use the opportunity to talk to a variety of people.

- Participate actively in an affinity group that reflects your foundation's interests and take advantage of the contacts they can provide (affinity groups with some degree of interest in Africa are listed in Appendix I).

- Attend conferences in Africa and elsewhere that will increase your knowledge about the countries and issues of interest to your foundation.

Bridging Cultural Differences

Africa is a continent of many different countries and often a multiplicity of cultures within each one. For Americans unfamiliar with Africa, cultural differences can be significant. They go beyond the obvious differences of language, food and social forms to more subtle differences in manners, expectations and how issues such as timing, distance, gender, money and power are perceived. Working effectively across cultures draws on personal qualities like sensitivity, open-mindedness, maturity, a caring for humanity and a sense of humor.

Experienced grantmakers suggest being patient, observing carefully, withholding judgment and asking questions that demonstrate heartfelt interest in learning about how other people behave and think. Listen carefully to what is being said and what is *not* being said. It is also a good idea to describe how your foundation operates internally and the kinds of government regulatory requirements the foundation must meet. By doing so, the grantee will better understand why certain questions are being asked and certain information requested.

At the same time, it is best to keep cultural differences in perspective. Many funders who have worked both domestically and in Africa point out that the issues around bridging cultures in Africa are not that different from working in diverse communities within the United States.

Keep in mind that culture shock can be a two-way street. African organizations, especially community-based groups and newer NGOs that have had little contact with foreign funders, can be intimidated by the expectations and directness of American foundation staff as well as the intricacies of the grantmaking process itself. It is important to keep in mind the often unacknowledged but crucial contributions of Africans to the grantmaking relationship like local knowledge and access to grassroots communities. A number of political, social and other factors may affect the extent to which Africans feel comfortable with speaking frankly with potential funders about certain topics, at least in the initial stage of a relationship. Africans may be selective about the kinds of information, such as personal or financial, they are willing to share based on cultural considerations.

Consequently, a high degree of sensitivity and diplomacy is essential to developing a trusting relationship with African organizations and it does not happen overnight. Gail McClure of the Kellogg Foundation counsels, "Be patient and persistent with both sides, with your own staff and boards, as well as with African partners, because you will have to be a leader in bringing them along. It's exhausting work. Learn to count to ten."

ADVICE BOX:

- Learn from more experienced grantmakers and NGOs that have worked successfully with Africans and African organizations.

- Hire African staff or consultants on a full-time, part-time or as-needed basis to liaise with African grantees.

- Consider starting off by funding in an English-speaking country (even though English may be a second or third language for many of its people).

- Listen carefully to what is being said and what is not being said.

- Explain how your foundation operates internally and why you need to ask your grantees the questions you do.

- Be open to new experiences and ways of thinking.

- Go slowly at first.

- Ask questions, listen and observe.

Achieving Sustainability

"Sustainability is another issue faced by both U.S. and Africa grantmakers," notes Andrea Johnson of the Carnegie Corporation of New York. She continues,

"We all want our grantees and their programs to last as long as the services are needed. However, the prospects for a nonprofit in the United States to diversify its resource base are greater than for its African counterpart. In the United States, individual donations and government contracts provide much of the income for the nonprofit sector as a whole. In African countries generally, governments have yet to embrace the concept that nongovernmental organizations can be effective providers of government-subsidized social services. Likewise, individual incomes are lower in Africa, and incentive systems for individuals are not yet in place in most countries to encourage private contributions to public causes on a scale large enough to sustain the not-for-profit sector. Thus, the risk of building dependence on foreign funders is very real."

Not all projects or organizations need to be sustained, but for many grantmakers, sustainability is a key long-term objective. Each grantmaker should determine how important sustainability is in its funding, then select grantee projects, programs or organizations that reflect this approach. Grantmakers should communicate their interest in sustainability early to potential grantees and work with them to maintain that focus.

"Sustainability is often defined in financial terms," reflects Monica Mutuku of the Kenya Community Development Foundation, "but it is really about the people." She encourages American foundations to go beyond "relief" as a short-term panacea and "to address the real needs of Africa… to empower people to handle their own problems and undertake their own development."

For many funders, a deterrent to making grants in Africa is a perceived lack of viable local institutions with which to partner. Many funders recognize the need to shore up the financial and management structure of small locally based, nonprofit groups in Africa in order to enhance their capacity to become more effective managers and activists. Foundations increasingly place an emphasis on the "organizational effectiveness" of their grant recipients while recognizing that basically sound organizations need to be strengthened in this area.

Many foundations make modest grants for projects to develop boards of directors, conduct long-range planning or improve internal management systems. Others make small planning grants as an initial form of assistance, helping potential grantees to further refine a project before full funding. Another approach is to allocate a certain percentage of project grant funding for the purpose of capacity-building. Still others have supported the development of indigenous philanthropy by helping to build community foundations and other locally based foundations in Africa. As noted earlier, Kresge has used challenge grants effectively as a means of fundraising building capacity at two South African universities.

Similarly, capacity-building is embedded in the W.K. Kellogg Foundation's approach to funding projects in the six southern African countries of Botswana, Lesotho, Mozambique, South Africa, Swaziland and Zimbabwe. The foundation's objective is to strengthen the capacity of Africans, their families, organizations and institutions to develop human capital, increase economic opportunity and improve civic participation in their communities, especially in rural areas.

The South Africa Program of the Rockefeller Brothers Fund (RBF) of New York City also includes an institutional strengthening and capacity-building component in the areas of basic education for children and adults and assistance for children made vulnerable by the HIV/AIDS pandemic. RBF makes capacity-building grants to both first-time and long-term partners and starts exploring institutional strengthening issues with each potential grantee early on in their relationship. A grant to the Thandanani Association to develop models for successful programs for AIDS orphans includes a capacity-building component that was negotiated during the grant review process. RBF grants to The Centre for Early Childhood Development and the Natal Adult Basic Education Support Trust also illustrate the foundation's capacity-building approach. Each of these organizations provides management training and organizational support to South African NGOs.

Finally, it may seem paradoxical to consider how a grantmaker might conclude its program while it is still planning its entry, but many grantmakers encourage early thinking on potential exit strategies. Even well-planned or successful initiatives almost always come to an end, and in some less positive cases, circumstances arise that truncate or alter a grantmaking strategy. Such alterations may come as a result of staff changes or new board initiatives on the part of the grantmaker or grantee, the vagaries of endowment returns, misunderstandings between the goals of the grantmaker and the capacity of the grantee, or evolving situations on the ground well beyond the control of either the grantmaker or the grantee. In general, African NGOs are more dependent on fewer sources of support, and are more vulnerable institutionally than their U.S. counterparts. How can the grantee find new funding sources to continue its important work after its grant ends? Mistakes happen and agendas change. How can a grantmaker best ensure that its grants leave its African grantee partners in a stronger position?

ADVICE BOX:

- Recognize that sustainability of projects and programs is a major challenge in Africa.

- Decide if sustainability is an important goal and work with grantees to develop an appropriate plan to achieve it.

- Understand that community self-help is a strong concept in Africa and that organized indigenous philanthropy is growing in many countries.

- Make challenge or matching grants.

- Fund through African community foundations.

- Include capacity-building in grants to African CBOs and NGOs, including strengthening fundraising capabilities.

- Introduce grantees to potential funding resources and donor networks.

- Publicize successful grants to attract new or additional funders.

- Consider potential exit or transition strategies.

Evaluating Progress and Measuring Impact

Experienced grantmakers rank measuring the impact of their funding in Africa as a high priority yet evaluation can be challenging even in the U.S. context, much less across barriers of language, culture, distance and unmatched expectations. For most, the process of evaluation and measuring impact is a collaborative one involving the grantmaker and the grantee as partners. Several grantmakers do not formally evaluate their grants, feeling that the process can undermine a collaborative relationship and intimidate grantees who are, in many cases, in the best position to know whether the grant is succeeding or not.

For those who do want to evaluate specific grants or grant programs, the key is starting before a grant is even made to develop the grantee measurement tools that are appropriate within the local context. Most of those interviewed for this book emphasize articulating clear, concrete indicators of success in the approved grant document, and they recommend that the grantee establish a good data baseline against which to measure the progress of the funded activity. However, it can take a considerable period of time for the full impact of a particular grant to be felt. "It's very hard to tell what the impact is — it takes years," cautions Nancy Muirhead of the Rockefeller Brothers Fund. "We bet on good people at the top of their fields, aiming for systemic change over time; there are so many variables."

One set of issues has to do with the capacity of the grantee organization to develop the baseline information and to track changes over time. Sometimes grantees need training or other technical assistance to enable them to design and implement the necessary measurement tools. These can be built into the grant. The United Nations Foundation actively encourages the U.N. to designate a percentage of each grant for evaluation purposes.

It is crucial that the grantee be as committed to the process as the funder, if not more so. If grantees view the evaluation or measurement process as serving the donor's needs and not their own, it will fail. Grantees must be persuaded that measuring and evaluating progress toward agreed upon goals reflects their own thinking and is meant to help them in their activities, not to punish them. A grantor-grantee relationship that is built on mutual trust is most likely to engender the confidence that grantees need to acknowledge less than positive results, learn from them and move on.

When Jennifer Astone, director of the Firelight Foundation, was involved in an evaluation with a nervous African grantee organization, she acknowledged that her foundation itself makes mistakes, too. The key point is to learn from mistakes rather than repeating them. The grantee organization, amazed at this admission, began to relax and view the evaluation exercise more as a collaborative learning experience. The Firelight Foundation also brought a group of its African grantees together and asked them to evaluate each other's grants, an exercise that proved to be a valuable learning experience for everyone involved.

In some cases the nature of the grant may not lend itself to quantitative measurement. "In some fields, results are clear," points out Gordon Perkin of the Bill & Melinda Gates Foundation. "When you vaccinate a child, you have been successful; in other areas which require significant behavior change, it's much more difficult to quantify success." Statistics, of course, do not tell the whole story. They are poor measures of, for example, hope or empowerment.

Yet, experienced grantmakers in Africa believe that even qualitative factors can be gauged through a process that involves a trusting learning environment with grantees, thinking through appropriate indicators of progress and looking for change in attitudes and behaviors over time. "The best thing you can do is help people to learn from each other, to nurture them so that they don't operate in a vacuum," says Andrea Gay with the U.N. Foundation.

The African Evaluation Association, an informal network facilitated by UNICEF's Eastern and Southern Africa Regional Office, has developed some resources that may be helpful to grantmakers in Africa, including evaluation guidelines and a checklist. See the resources section in Appendix I for contact information.

- Think of evaluation as a learning tool for both grantmaker and grantee; make it a collaboration.

- Decide early on if an evaluation would be useful; not all grants merit evaluation.

- Work with grantees to identify appropriate indicators of success.

- Establish baseline data against which the grant can be measured.

- Think creatively of ways to measure qualitative factors that cannot be captured by statistics.

- Bear in mind that it may not be cost-effective to evaluate individual small grants although they might be evaluated on a group basis.

- Build a sense of trust and confidence with grantees so that they feel comfortable acknowledging problem grants and learning from them.

- Admit mistakes as grantmakers; use them to illustrate to grantees the learning value of evaluation.

- Make grantee evaluation of the *grantmaker* a part of the overall evaluation process.

CHAPTER 9

Examples of Foundation and Corporate Grants in Africa

"What is sown will sprout."
(Oromo proverb from Ethiopia and Kenya)

This chapter highlights examples that illustrate the wide range of approach, focus, size and type of grants that foundations and corporations are making in Africa. While the funded activities vary greatly, and it is too early to assess their long-term impact, some common elements enhance the potential for successful outcomes:

- identification and thoughtful analysis of a locally identified need;

- consultation with local people and organizations about how best to meet that need;

- selection of organizations with strong leadership and clear vision;

- willingness to start with general support and capacity-building assistance if needed;

- maintaining good communication to build a trusting and respectful relationship with grantees over time;

- beginning with a clear plan but adapting to changing circumstances;

- a long-term perspective and commitment; and

- creative partnerships with other grantmakers, businesses and governments that maximize the advantages of each sector.

American Express — Employment Training in Travel and Tourism/South Africa

The American Express Company in New York gives ongoing support through its Global Travel & Tourism Partnership to the National Business Initiative, a South African nonprofit, to operate a program providing elective courses and practical experience through provincial schools for high school students interested in working in the travel and tourism industry. Tourism is viewed as one of South Africa's growth industries, one that can help address the country's high unemployment rate. The program is the first industry course to be accepted by the South African Government as part of the national school curriculum. Beginning as a pilot project in 1996, after seven years the program is now available to 40,000 students in 368 schools throughout the country. American Express pays for the program director's salary.

Edna McConnell Clark Foundation — Preventing and Treating Trachoma-Related Blindness/Morocco

Trachoma is a contagious infection of the eyelids and the leading cause of preventable blindness in the world, with especially high incidence among women and children living under conditions of poverty. Based on its long-standing support for tropical disease research, the Edna McConnell Clark Foundation of New York City, in partnership with the pharmaceutical company Pfizer Inc., established the International Trachoma Initiative (ITI) in 1999 dedicated to the elimination of trachoma-related blindness. ITI's campaign includes several components: surgery for the advanced stages of the disease, the use of antibiotics donated by Pfizer to treat active infections, education programs to encourage personal hygiene, and community programs to improve access to clean water and sanitation facilities. One of the countries targeted by the International Trachoma Initiative is Morocco where ITI is partnering with the Ministry of Health and the Ministry of Education. The Edna McConnell Clark Foundation made a grant of $26,500 to ITI for the Fondation Hassan II d'Ophtalmologie in Rabat, Morocco to support the surgery component of the program in the southern region of that country from May 2001 through August 2004.

The Firelight Foundation — Bakery Project Employing AIDS Orphans/Rwanda

In 2001, the Firelight Foundation of Santa Cruz, California, made a $13,400 grant to the Association des Femmes Chefs de Famille (Association of Women Heads of Households) in the Giribanga community of Kigali, Rwanda's capital city, to operate a bakery that employs AIDS orphans. The association, known as AFCF, began as an income-generating program for widows of the 1994 genocide and the AIDS epidemic, struggling to support their own households as well as extended families. With the number of child-headed households in the community growing due to AIDS, AFCF established a bakery in 2001 with the Firelight grant. The grant funded the equipment, personnel and raw materials to start the bakery in addition to a five-day training program for 100 children in a variety of income-generating activities as well as legal and human rights. Eighteen youths were trained for the bakery and are earning their first regular income to support their families. In 2002 Firelight made a $4,000 grant to AFCF to hire technical assistance to develop a marketing and training plan for expanding the youth-run bakery.

The Ford Foundation/Rockefeller Foundation/ Aga Khan Foundation — Building Indigenous Philanthropy/Kenya

Faced with Kenya's worsening development problems and an extensive NGO sector largely dependent on external donors, The Ford Foundation began exploring a new, more sustainable model for community development in that country in the late 1990s. After several years of consultations with community-based organizations and NGOs in Kenya, the Kenya Community Development Foundation (KCDF) was launched in 1997 as a project of the Aga Khan Foundation with financial support from Ford. The mission of KCDF is to create a Kenyan foundation that effectively mobilizes resources from private and public sources and builds permanent funds for grantmaking for the development of communities throughout the country. KCDF became an independent organization in 2001 and received a $87,000 grant that year from the Rockefeller Foundation for research aimed at raising awareness of indigenous philanthropy in Kenya. Ford provided funds for technical assistance for KCDF as well as funding for both operating and program costs. In addition, Ford linked the KCDF staff to other community foundations in Africa and in the United States. Today, KCDF makes grants ranging from $1,000 to $20,000 to strengthen the capacity-building and sustainability of community-based organizations throughout Kenya. In 2003, Ford Foundation made a new grant of $650,000 to the Kenya Community Development Foundation for general support, management and governance, asset development, and an additional grant to establish a scholarship fund.

The Global Fund for Women —
Disabled Women Entrepreneurs/Uganda

The Global Fund for Women in San Francisco supported Whirlwind Women of Whirlwind Wheelchair International, a women's wheelchair-building project at San Francisco State University, with an initial $5,000 grant in 1999 to train three disabled Ugandan women for a wheelchair-building project in the capital city Kampala. As a result of the grant, Mobility Appliances for Disabled Women Entrepreneurs (MADE) was created as a Ugandan NGO. The organization's mission is to train and employ disabled women in the production and maintenance of wheelchairs from locally available materials. Thirty women are now employed in the project, which generates income for them, builds their independence, meets an urgent social need, and breaks downs stereotypes around what women and disabled people can achieve. The Global Fund for Women followed its first grant with a two-year grant of $30,000 to support and expand the work of MADE from 2001–2003.

Global Greengrants Fund — Campaign to Protect the Cross River Forest/Nigeria

The Global Greengrants Fund in Boulder, Colorado, made numerous grants to a Nigerian NGO environmental coalition called NGOCE, the Nigerian NGO Coalition for the Environment (NGOCE). When Nigeria's biologically rich Cross River Forest was threatened with extensive logging by a Hong Kong corporation working with Nigeria's then military regime in 1997, Global Greengrants made a small grant of $3,000 to NGOCE to support community organizing and international publicity to stop the environmental threat. The campaign led to a temporary moratorium on logging and creation of a Forestry Commission to explore better ways to develop the resources of the Cross River Forest. Odhigha Odigha, the environmental activist who heads NGOCE, serves as one of two NGO representatives on the Forestry Commission's board. Global Greengrants made subsequent grants of $1,400 and $5,800 to NGOCE for materials, equipment and Earth Day activities to continue the campaign to protect the Cross River Forests.

Conrad N. Hilton Foundation — West Africa Water Initiative/Ghana-Mali-Niger

Guinea worm, trachoma and diarrheal disease pose serious health threats in much of Africa, including the tropical West Africa region. The Conrad N. Hilton Foundation of Los Angeles made grants totaling nearly $14 million since 1990 to World Vision's Ghana affiliate to eradicate the guinea worm and provide access to clean drinking water as part of the Ghana Rural Water Project. That effort, which has been focused on isolated villages in Ghana, expanded in 2002 to encompass rural areas of Mali and Niger as well. The broader West Africa Water Initiative, as it is now known, builds on the experience in Ghana and Hilton's long-term relationship with World Vision while incorporating the participation of established partners such as the Desert Research Institute, Cornell University, The Carter Center, Helen Keller Worldwide as well as new partnerships with UNICEF, WaterAid, Winrock and Lions Clubs International. The Hilton Foundation made a new commitment of nearly $18 million over seven years to the three-country initiative. The multifaceted project includes drilling boreholes, sanitation and hygiene education. Today, the project benefits nearly half a million people.

The Kresge Foundation — Challenge Grants to Build University Fundraising Capacity/South Africa

The Kresge Foundation of Troy, Michigan, made two challenge grants to the University of Cape Town in South Africa. In 1989, Kresge made a $500,000 challenge grant for the construction of a nonracial student residence hall. Ten years later, encouraged by the success of its first grant, Kresge made a $1.5 million challenge grant for renovation of the University of Cape Town's central library and renovation of its upper campus. The university had already raised a significant amount of funding toward the project, and Kresge required it to raise an additional $4 million in new private gifts within a 15-month period in order to receive the challenge grant. Ultimately, the university's fundraising exceeded the challenge grant's goal, it completed its project, and the university expanded its donor base and internal fundraising capacity in the process.

John D. and Catherine T. MacArthur Foundation — Sexuality Education in the Schools/Nigeria

The John D. and Catherine T. MacArthur Foundation in Chicago has supported a Nigerian NGO Action Health Incorporated since 1990. At first, Action Health was a small organization struggling to define its mission. As it grew, the organization developed a focus on adolescent health issues in view of Nigeria's burgeoning teenage population and the spread of HIV/AIDS. Taking a multi-dimensional approach involving education, training, health services and research, Action Health has become an influential advocate for sexuality education for young people in Nigeria. In 2001, the MacArthur Foundation made a three-year grant of $350,000 to Action Health for a project to increase young people's access to sexuality education in one region of the country.

Action Health now works in 80 Nigerian schools bringing sexuality education programs directly to young people. The work of the organization is having an even wider impact since, due in part to the efforts of Action Health, Nigeria's Department of Education approved a national sexuality education curriculum.

The McKnight Foundation — Support for Community Foundation/Zimbabwe

The McKnight Foundation of Minneapolis made a two-year grant of $170,000 in 2000 to the New York-based Synergos Institute to support the work of the Community Foundation for the Western Region of Zimbabwe. Synergos helped a Zimbabwean grassroots NGO, the Organization for Rural Associations for Progress, to establish the community foundation in 1992 with contributions from international donors and 50,000 villagers in Zimbabwe's impoverished western area. Against a backdrop of growing political authoritarianism, inflation, economic instability and drought, the McKnight grant is enabling the community foundation to expand its work with community leaders to stabilize and strengthen local associations and women's groups that are working to improve the quality of life for women and their families in Zimbabwe's western region.

Merck & Co., Inc., The Merck Company Foundation and the Bill & Melinda Gates Foundation — Comprehensive HIV/AIDS Program/Botswana

In Botswana, one out of every three adults is infected with HIV and the number of AIDS-related deaths has tripled since 1995. To address the problem, Merck & Co. and the Merck Company Foundation in Whitehouse Station, New Jersey, are collaborating with the Bill & Melinda Gates Foundation in Seattle, the Harvard AIDS Institute in Boston, the Government of Botswana and others on a comprehensive HIV/AIDS partnership in Botswana. The five-year, $100 million project has set a goal of improving the entire spectrum of HIV prevention, care and treatment in Botswana. Half of the project's funding comes from Merck with the other half from Gates. The Merck Company is also donating its two AIDS medications. The project supports a comprehensive strategy of education, prevention, treatment and care. The strategy was developed by the Government of Botswana and is implemented through its National AIDS Coordinating Agency and Ministry of Health. Efforts to address the AIDS epidemic in Botswana are requiring the project to improve the infrastructure of Botswana's healthcare delivery system and to partner with community-based and private sector organizations to develop and implement HIV/AIDS education, prevention and care programs.

Charles Stewart Mott Foundation — Rural Empowerment/South Africa

The C.S. Mott Foundation of Flint, Michigan, began supporting the Social Change Assistance Trust (SCAT) in Cape Town, South Africa, in 1995. SCAT is an independent fundraising and grantmaking development agency founded under apartheid in 1985 with a mission of empowering the rural poor, strengthening civil society and promoting social change. Mott's first two-year grant of $300,000 supported SCAT's Fundraising Incentive Scheme which rewards community efforts to address local needs by matching funds raised locally on a five to one basis. Fundraising events include disco nights, sports tournaments, chorale competitions, public video viewings, raffles, bake sales and other activities. Based on the initial success of the fundraising incentive program, Mott gave a second $300,000 grant to SCAT in 1998, part of which was used for organizational development of the trust and some regranting to local community organizations. SCAT now works through advice offices in four of South Africa's nine provinces, providing skill training for local development agencies as well as training for their volunteer committees. In 2000, the Mott Foundation made a third grant of $300,000 to the Social Change Assistance Trust to analyze grantmaking trends and their impact.

Mulago Foundation — Boosting Income for Small-holder Farmers/Kenya

In 2001, the Mulago Foundation of San Francisco made a $200,000 grant to a Kenyan NGO called ApproTEC to help small-holder farmers grow second or third vegetable crops by using manual irrigation pumps. The project initiated a virtual cascade of development. With the low-cost treadle-type pumps, crops can be grown throughout the year and can be brought to market during the off-season when prices are high. As a result, farmers participating in the project have increased their incomes by as much as ten times. With an investment of $50, farmers can earn $1,000 for education and healthcare. The pumps are manufactured locally in Kenya and Tanzania, and sold through retailers in the two countries, creating 16,000 new jobs. A total of 24,000 pumps are in use, generating $3.8 million in new income per year.

CHAPTER 10

Insights from Experienced Grantmakers . . . in Their Own Words

"She who knows the path is she who travels it." (Zulu proverb from South Africa)

BISI ADELEYE-FAYEMI — *Executive Director, African Women's Development Fund in Ghana*

The African Women's Development Fund raises funds and makes grants to African organizations in support of women's human rights, political participation, peace-building, economic empowerment, reproductive rights, health and HIV/AIDS.

⁁ Tap into Africa's vibrant civil society. ⁁

"I think one of the first things grantmakers interested in supporting work in Africa should do is talk to others who have had more experience in the field. By doing this, you learn from the successes and challenges of others. International peer networks such as the Africa Grantmakers' Affinity Group, Grantmakers Without Borders, International Human Rights Funders Group and International Network of Women's Funds, to name just a few, are very important sources of information and expertise. In addition to this, establishing contact with local grantmakers within Africa is very important. Local grantmakers are not just 'intermediary' or 're-granting' entities. They bring a whole lot more to the philanthropic table, such as unique insights, networks, innovative grantmaking strategies and sound knowledge of the local context. From our experience of grantmaking in Africa, I would also like to mention the following:

1. Respect and trust are very important.

2. Successful grantmaking in Africa involves investments in institutional capacity-building. You should also be prepared to stick around for longer than just one year.

3. Do not have unrealistic expectations of the reach of your dollars. Many things are actually more expensive in Africa due to the fledgling infrastructure, such as communications, electricity, transport, etc.

4. Try to involve grantees in your foundation policy discussions and reviews.

5. The challenges that Africa faces cannot be solved by 'big spenders' alone. Every little bit counts. Decide on an issue, theme or country and do what you can.

"There is a vibrant civil society across the continent, which has kept many states together when everything else has collapsed. Through the strategic use of grantmaking networks, Africa field offices of established grantmakers, and local grantmakers, you can find the information you need."

CHRIS ALLAN — *Associate Director, Global Greengrants Fund*

The Global Greengrants Fund makes small grants to grassroots groups working toward environmental health, justice and sustainability in Africa and other developing regions.

Support organizations that engage policymakers to bring about social change.

"Given the vast and growing differences between the economies of the United States and most African countries, it is not difficult to justify grantmaking in Africa. What is harder is to decide what is effective and to find an efficient means of achieving results. After several decades of grantmaking, most foundation staff can tell you what approaches have worked better than others, and which sectors show the most promise. But in general, the most promising and broad-reaching development in the last decade has been the opening in most places of a broad-thinking civil society sector that is able to link grassroots organizing with national and international policy. The frustration of the past was the all-too-common scenario when the results of a terrific local tomato-growing project were wiped out overnight by sudden changes in national or international policy, with no notice, debate or public input.

"The most exciting development has been the emergence of a plethora of organizations that are working to bring about social change at all levels — local, national and international. The challenge for donors is to support these forward-looking people to 1) continue to engage policymakers and to challenge them to develop real policies in the public interest, and 2) help them to develop further roots in civil society that give them a democratic grounding. It is astonishing what these brave people can achieve on ridiculously skimpy and unreliable budgets. Continued, thoughtful, reliable and long-term funding for this work from Northern donors can make a world of difference both in individual communities and across entire societies."

Carol Berde — *Executive Vice President, The McKnight Foundation*

The McKnight Foundation makes small grants for women's economic and social empowerment in Zimbabwe, Tanzania and Uganda.

 Maintain an active presence in-country.

"After a decade of Africa grantmaking, four lessons are continually reinforced for us at McKnight. First, identify your strategies and boundaries and stick to them. There are always compelling needs, but we can be more effective if we concentrate resources. Second, maintain an active presence in-country. That doesn't have to mean an office, but it does mean frequent trips to the region. Third, build, maintain and use your networks. The greatest advantage of regular visits to Africa is the network of people and organizations you build and use to keep informed. Fourth, be prepared for everything and don't assume anything."

Dyanne Hayes — *Vice President, Programs, Conrad N. Hilton Foundation*

The Conrad N. Hilton Foundation is a major funder of a large multi-partner seven-year program to provide clean water to rural people in the West African countries of Ghana, Mali and Niger.

Focus, focus, focus.

"As the sporting manufacturer admonishes . . . Just Do It! Your grants don't have to be in the multi-millions to make an enormous difference, yet you must be clear in what you want to achieve. Focus, focus, focus geographically and programmatically. Regardless of the issue or the problem, identify one aspect, an unfilled niche that needs attention, at which to target your resources and be willing to stick with it; i.e., a five to 10-year commitment."

1. From the beginning, project ideas require local involvement — the project must be community-based, community-driven and community-managed. Insist on the inclusion of women in all facets of planning and operations.

2. An integrated programmatic approach is essential; i.e., skills development, education and training to build local capacity at the village, district and national levels.

3. All technology involved (in this case, the hardware for boreholes and latrines and hand pumps and spare parts for repair) must be affordable, manageable and easily accessible so as to ensure long-term sustainability."

ANDREA JOHNSON — *Program Officer, Carnegie Corporation of New York*

The Carnegie Corporation of New York makes large multi-year grants to public institutions and smaller support grants for private nonprofits in a number of African countries to strengthen universities, enhance women's opportunities in higher education and revitalize public libraries.

Build management and fundraising capacity.

"Africa grantmakers face issues similar to those encountered by their U.S.-focused colleagues. These issues, however, tend to be magnified in Africa, and the options for addressing them are not necessarily straightforward. For example, U.S. grantmakers working with community-based organizations are often faced with the dilemma of weak institutional infrastructure and management. This situation is mirrored in Africa — strong subject specialists who have little management experience or training lead organizations where management and organizational capacity-building receive little attention and few financial resources. While the nonprofit support sector in the United States — which provides training and consulting services on a range of management and organizational development themes for nonprofit managers — has grown over the years, opportunities in most African countries are much more limited. This presents a challenge to Africa grantmakers who want to see their grantee organizations build their capacity to use their scarce resources — human, financial, and material — to the utmost effect. High quality local training and consulting resources might not be available, and 'imported' expertise might not be relevant, so imagination and ingenuity are required.

"Does this mean that grantmakers should avoid Africa? Of course not. Dollar for dollar, we can probably make a greater difference in the lives of individuals in Africa than we can in the lives of Americans, where money is in greater supply. We just have to keep the African contexts (plural, because conditions vary across the countries) in mind and adjust our grantmaking strategies accordingly. At Carnegie Corporation, we are trying to do this by developing a technical assistance track for our university partners in Africa. In addition to the direct support they receive to strengthen their capacity for teaching and research —understandably their top priority — we are also developing opportunities for them to build their management and fundraising capacity. Since our support can't last forever, our objective is to help strengthen the universities in multiple ways so that they can replace our support and expand their resources over time."

GAIL MCCLURE — *Vice President for Programs,*
W.K. Kellogg Foundation

The W.K. Kellogg Foundation makes both large and small
grants to strengthen Africans, their families, organizations
and institutions as they work to develop and sustain healthy
communities in six countries of the Southern Africa region.

Hire Africans as professional program staff and form a two-way learning partnership with African grantees.

"For over 25 years, the Kellogg Foundation has staffed its international offices
in southern Africa and elsewhere with professionals from the countries where
it has programs. We have found that our approach of giving the leadership for
the program to the people of the region helps to keep us firmly grounded in
our mission of 'helping people help themselves' wherever we go. We Americans
tend to be pragmatic by nature and technologically inclined. That often has us
leaning toward 'fixing' things and applying models that have worked for us in
our own development or what we have seen work in other places. While we
agree that sharing and exposure can be highly beneficial, we think that local
people need to do the decisionmaking around relevance and adaptation —
with our assistance and advice. So to borrow a phrase from the educators, we
try to be 'the guide at the side' rather than the 'sage on the stage' and form a
true learning partnership with others.

"Kellogg's commitment to staffing and working with host country or regional
nationals keeps us true to our mission of empowering people in communities to
solve their own problems. It also helps the foundation avoid many of the pitfalls
of development work (e.g. excessive paternalism, dependency, etc). This approach
can certainly be time-consuming and pose a number of challenges. Is it worth
it? We think so. And as Americans trying to learn to be good global citizens, it
helps us to grow and develop."

 **CHRIS MKHIZE** — *Director, Uthungulu Community Foundation in South Africa*

The Uthungulu Community Foundation raises funds and makes grants for education, health, agriculture and small business development projects in the Zululand area of South Africa.

⁀ Work toward sustainability of projects. ⁀

"In the Uthungulu Community Foundation's interactions with potential international donors, they would generally not be keen to make donations to local communities or organizations where there appears to be no prospect for sustainability of initiated projects. Equally, potential donors, including the World Bank, would like to form development partnerships only with countries and organizations that demonstrate that structures are in place for community participation in development programs, and where there would be some professional, effective and efficient management and administration systems as well as public accountability, democratization processes and collaboration between and among private and public sector organizations.

"The Uthungulu Community Foundation, in the process of issuing grants to targeted local communities, makes no secret of the fact that issued grants are based on socio-economic values of sustainability, self-reliance, accountable management and self-development. For sustainability of grants, local communities must have ways and means of collecting required funds from other sources rather than depend solely on the foundation. Once local communities have been assisted with seed funding for a period of maybe three to five years, one would expect such communities to stand on their own."

KERRY OLSON — *President and Founder, Firelight Foundation*

The Firelight Foundation makes small grants to grassroots organizations that provide direct assistance to vulnerable children affected by HIV/AIDS.

Don't underestimate the power of small grants that support local solutions to local problems.

"Firelight Foundation supports the needs of children orphaned and affected by AIDS in Sub-Saharan Africa. In our first three years of operation, we supported over 100 community-based organizations serving children and families in 11 African countries. The single most important lesson we have learned is: never underestimate the power of small grants given at the grassroots level. Dollars invested in community-based initiatives can have great impact — not only in the lives of children and their families, but also on the overall capacity of communities to address their own needs.

"In the Butula District of western Kenya the adult prevalence of AIDS (30 percent) has had devastating effects on children and the community. An initial grant from Firelight enabled the Rural Education and Economic Enhancement Program (REEP) to provide youth heading households with skills training and micro-credit loans for caregivers, most of whom are HIV-positive women and elderly persons. In just over three years, the community's attitude toward people living with AIDS has been transformed. Previously, the stigma of AIDS was so great that those who thought they were infected simply gave up hope, and many affected children were left uncared for. Now, the community is characterized by hope, AIDS awareness, and an increased commitment and capacity within families to provide and care for vulnerable children.

"Many community initiatives with as much promise as REEP are never funded, simply because so few dollars make it to the community level. Supporting community responses require a willingness to engage in responsible risk-taking, an ability to make smaller grants, and an underlying respect for local leaders. Firelight has learned a great deal from our African grantee-partners and has found that community-based programs and ideas are influencing the way nations tackle the issues of HIV/AIDS. While there is a place and a need for funding at all levels, we have found that supporting local solutions to local problems is both effective and empowering."

 **KATHARINE PEARSON** — *former Ford Foundation Representative, East Africa Office*

The Ford Foundation's grantmaking program in East Africa provides modest grants and technical assistance in the areas of community development, asset building and strengthening indigenous philanthropy.

Develop the assets of African organizations.

1. "It is really possible to work with existing organizations; it's not necessary to create something new.

2. In Africa, there's a thin level of technical assistance and expertise to do the work. It's not enough to have the money coming in. It's important to build the institutions so they become grantmakers themselves.

3. To do long-term development, a foundation must be facile in making small grants of $500, $1,000 or $2,000. Small grantmaking is absolutely crucial and big foundations cannot do this themselves; they have to work with local organizations.

4. Learning is a two-way street. It's an exchange. African grantmakers have a contribution to make back to U.S. foundations.

5. A foundation can only see if an effort will be sustainable over a 5–7 year period. All this stuff takes a long time. It's not one grant."

DANIEL ROBBINS, M.D. — *Executive Officer, J.F. Kapnek Charitable Trust/Pediatric AIDS Foundation - Zimbabwe*

The J.F. Kapnek Charitable Trust/Pediatric AIDS Foundation makes small grants for biomedical research and HIV prevention programs focused on women and children in Zimbabwe.

⁀ Be consistent and think long-term. ⁀

"There are many messages which resonate as important to grantmaking in Africa, most of which are relevant to grantmaking anywhere. The one thing I would share as the element that has been of particular importance to grantmaking and program development in Zimbabwe, for the Kapnek Trust, has been our temporal consistency. The fact that we have been involved in philanthropic activity in the region for nearly 50 years has been of great value. I believe the cornerstone of our success has been our staying power: whether in negotiations with Ministry of Health officials, working with local partner organizations or speaking with volunteers on our scholarship committee, the fact that all involved know our commitment is for the long term seems to enable great things to happen time and time again.

"I would encourage those interested in getting involved in grantmaking in Africa to consider developing a long-term strategy if appropriate. If not, then seek a partner who has been involved in the immediate area for some time. Whether direct or indirect, the value of this temporal consistency will greatly enhance your effectiveness and make the experience more meaningful for all involved. It is the best general advice I can give for those exploring this rewarding endeavor."

Appendix I: *Helpful Resources for Grantmaking in Africa*

The resources available to grantmakers interested in learning about Africa and opportunities for funding there are far more extensive than can be listed in this publication. Following is a general list of organizations, publications and websites that may be helpful in getting started.

Grantmaker Affinity Groups

Africa Grantmakers' Affinity Group (www.agag.org) is the only affinity group with a specific focus on Africa.

The following affinity groups work on global issues and have an interest in Africa:

Environmental Grantmakers Association (www.ega.org)

Funders Concerned About AIDS (www.fcaaids.org)

Funders Network on Population, Reproductive Health and Rights (www.fundersnet.org)

Funders Network on Trade and Globalization (www.fntg.org)

Grantmakers Without Borders (www.gwob.org)

International Funders for Indigenous People (www.internationalfunders.org)

International Human Rights Funders Group (www.hrfunders.org)

International Network of Women's Funds (www.inwf.org)

Women's Funding Network (www.wfnet.org)

Nonprofit Resources

Africa Action (www.africaaction.org)

Africa-America Institute (www.aaionline.org)

Africare (www.africare.org)

Africa Faith and Justice Network (www.afjn.org)

Africa Studies Association (www.africanstudies.org)

Africa Women's Development Fund (www.awdf.org)

African Evaluation Association (www.afrea.org)

Bread for the World (www.bread.org)

The Carter Center (www.cartercenter.org)

CIVICUS: World Alliance for Citizen Participation (www.civicus.org)

Council on Foundations (www.cof.org)

Corporate Council on Africa (www.africacncl.org)

Global Philanthropy Forum (www.philanthropyforum.org)

Grantcraft: Practical Wisdom for Grantmakers (www.grantcraft.org)

Human Rights Watch Africa (www.hrw.org/africa)

InterAction (www.interaction.org)

International Center for Not-for-Profit Law (www.icnl.org)

Kenya Community Development Foundation (www.kcdfoundation.org)

National Summit on Africa (www.africasummit.org)

New Partnership for Africa's Development (www.nepad.org)

South Africa Institute for Advancement (www.inyathelo.co.za)

Synergos Institute (www.synergos.org)

TransAfrica (www.transafricaforum.org)

Transparency International (www.transparency.org)

U.S. International Grantmaking (USIG) (www.usig.org)

Ufadhili, The Centre for Philanthropy and Social Responsibility, a regional
organization covering Kenya, Tanzania and Uganda (www.ufadhilitrust.org)

Worldwide Initiatives for Grantmaker Support (WINGS) (www.wingsweb.org)

Multilateral Organizations

African Development Bank (www.afdb.org)

United Nations Specialized Agencies (www.un.org)

    Convention to Combat Desertification (CCD) (www.unccd.int)

    U.N. Economic Commission for Africa (UNECA) (www.uneca.org)

    World Health Organization (WHO) (www.who.int)

    UNAIDS (www.unaids.org)

    U.N. Development Programme (UNDP) (www.undp.org)

    U.N. Economic, Social and Cultural Organization (UNESCO) (www.unesco.org)

    U.N. Fund for Population Activities (UNFPA) (www.unfpa.org)

    U.N. Children's Emergency Fund (UNICEF) (www.unicef.org)

    U.N. Fund for International Partnerships (UNFIP) (www.un.org/unfip)

    U.N. High Commissioner for Refugees (UNHCR) (www.unhcr.ch)

    U.N. Environment Program (UNEP) (www.unep.org)

World Bank (www.worldbank.org)

    Africa Programs (www.worldbank.org/afr/)

    African Development Indicators 2006, The World Bank, 2006.

    Atlas of Global Development: A Visual Guide to the World's Greatest Challenges, The World Bank and Harper Collins, 2007.

U.S. Government

African Development Foundation (www.adf.gov)

U.S. Agency for International Development (www.usaid.gov)
   Africa (www.usaid.gov/locations/sub-saharan_africa)
   Global Development Alliance (www.usaid.gov/gda)

U.S. Treasury Department Office of Foreign Assets Control
   (www.treasury.gov/ofac)

Publications

Beyond Our Borders: A Guide to Making Grants Outside the United States by
John A. Edie and Jane C. Nober, Council on Foundations, 1999.

Disaster Grantmaking: A Practical Guide for Foundations and Corporations,
Council on Foundations and European Foundation Centre, 2007.

Expenditure Responsibility Step by Step , Third Edition, by John A. Edie, Council
on Foundations, 2005.

Grantmaking Basics: A Field Guide for Funders by Barbara D. Kibbe, Fred
Setterberg and Colburn S. Wilbur with Jan Masaoka, Council on Foundations,
1999.

Grantmaking in an Age of Terrorism: Some Thoughts About Compliance Strategies
by Janne G. Gallagher, Council on Foundations, 2004.

*Handbook on Counter-Terrorism Measures: What U.S. Nonprofits and
Grantmakers Need to Know*, "Legal Dimensions of International Grantmaking
Series" 2nd quarter, 2004, by The Council on Foundations, Independent
Sector, InterAction and Day, Berry & Howard Foundation.

Hope At Last, A Guide to Grantmaking in South Africa by Dr. Michael R.
Sinclair, Henry J. Kaiser Foundation, 1990.

Other Resources

AllAfrica (allafrica.com)

M-Web Africa (mwebafrica.com)

Africa Confidential (www.africa-confidential.com)

Appendix II: *Brief Overview of Africa's Five Major Regions*

North Africa

Comprised of Algeria, Egypt, Libya, Morocco, Tunisia and the disputed area known as Western Sahara, North Africa is distinguished from the rest of the continent, which is collectively referred to as sub-Saharan Africa. The North Africa region is bordered on the north by the Mediterranean Sea and on the south by the Sahara Desert. The main language of the region is Arabic although French and Berber, an indigenous language, are also used in Algeria and Morocco. Islam is the major religion of the region except for Morocco's more indigenous Arab-Berber religion. With over 70 million people, Egypt is the region's most populous country. Algeria and Morocco each have populations of about 30 million people spread across desert, mountain and coastal zones. Oil and agricultural products are the main exports of the region. Islam is the principal religion of North Africa with fundamentalist insurgent groups threatening governments in both Egypt and Algeria. Morocco is a constitutional monarchy. Democracy is not strongly rooted in the region; Algeria is struggling to maintain an elected parliamentary form of government.

Not surprisingly, the economic and political orientation of North African countries tends to be toward the Middle East and Europe rather than sub-Saharan Africa. North Africa, as a whole, is relatively better off than sub-Saharan Africa. None of the countries of North Africa qualifies as a low-income country (annual income of $745 or less per capita) according to World Bank standards. While poverty is certainly a reality in the region, less than 2 percent of the population in Algeria, Morocco and Tunisia live on less than $1 per day. For Egypt, the figure is even lower at .5 percent of the population. At the same time, literacy among girls and women is actually declining. Building and strengthening civil society organizations, promoting democracy, gender equity and extending basic education, especially for girls, are some of the major developmental concerns for the region.

West Africa

The West African region is comprised of 16 countries located on the continent's large western bulge into the Atlantic Ocean. Much of the region was colonized by France (Benin, Burkina Faso, Chad, Ivory Coast, Mali, Mauritania, Niger, Senegal, Togo), Britain (Gambia, Ghana, Nigeria, Sierra Leone) and Portugal (Cape Verde, Guinea Bissau). As a result, English, French and Portuguese are widely spoken in the former colonies as well as Arabic and a multitude of indigenous languages like Wolof in Senegal, Yoruba in Nigeria and Bambara in Mali. Because of this cultural mix, it is not unusual for Africans to speak three, four or even five different languages.

For three centuries, the slave trade operated from the ports of West Africa to North and South America and the West Indies. Liberia, where English is spoken along with indigenous languages, was founded by freed American slaves in 1847.

Islam, Christianity (both Roman Catholic and Protestant) and indigenous belief systems provide a different religious mix in each country of West Africa with Islam generally stronger in northern areas bordering on the Sahara Desert. The region's chief exports, often controlled by multinational corporations using African labor, include agricultural products such as cotton, textiles, palm oil, ground nuts, cocoa, coffee and rubber, as well as minerals like gold, iron ore, bauxite and diamonds. With 130 million people, Nigeria is Africa's most populous country and perhaps one of its wealthiest, due to substantial oil and natural gas deposits. Nigeria is also struggling with cultural and political conflict between its Muslim north and non-Muslim south. In 2001, a controversial $3.7 billion World Bank-funded pipeline was approved linking oil deposits in Chad to offshore oil-loading facilities on Cameroon's Atlantic coast.

Some of Africa's poorest countries are located in West Africa. In Mali, for instance, nearly 73 percent of the population lives on less than $1 a day. And in Nigeria, despite it oil resources, 70 percent of the population lives on less than $1 a day. Burkina Faso, Chad, and the Gambia are also among Africa's poorest countries. The Economic Community of West African States (ECOWAS) was formed in 1975 to facilitate greater integration of the region's national economies, which historically have tended to be linked to former colonial rulers rather than with each other. Maintaining agricultural and livestock production for small-holder farmers in this drought-prone region; protecting fragile river, forest and farming ecosystems against deforestation and encroachment by the Sahara Desert; and developing oil and mineral resources in ways that bring broad public benefit are some of the development challenges facing this region.

Central Africa

Central Africa is comprised of Burundi, Cameroon, Central African Republic, Republic of the Congo (Brazzaville), Equatorial Guinea, Democratic Republic of Congo (formerly Zaire), Gabon, Rwanda and the island nation of Sao Tome & Principe. Although sparsely populated compared with other regions of Africa, Central Africa is blessed with abundant natural resources like oil, diamonds, copper, nickel, uranium and cobalt. Unfortunately, these resources in the region's dominant country, the Democratic Republic of Congo, made it a prime target for colonial exploitation, then superpower manipulation during the Cold War, followed by economic plundering by the corrupt regime of deposed dictator Mobutu Sese Seko.

Moreover, colonial legacies, ethnic strife, and increasing poverty have generated instability in the region such as that which resulted in the 1994 genocide in

Rwanda. That conflict spawned massive internal displacement and cross-border refugees from both Rwanda and Burundi into neighboring Uganda, Tanzania and the Democratic Republic of Congo (DRC) where a civil war was already under way. The DRC, previously known as Zaire and before that the Belgian Congo, dominates the region because of its geographic size and population of nearly 53 million people. Due to the extensive colonial influence of Belgium in the Central Africa region, French is the principal language although many indigenous languages including Swahili, Bantu, and others are spoken depending on the locale. Christianity (both Roman Catholic and Protestant) is well-established in the region, accounting for the religion of more than half the population in Gabon, Rwanda and the Democratic Republic of Congo. Indigenous religions rank second, with Islam playing a relatively minor role in this region.

The Central Africa region boasts some of the continent's most precious — and threatened — natural resources, including the biodiversity-rich rainforests of Cameroon and Gabon, the Congo River and endangered species such as Rwanda's famous gorillas. Poverty rates in the region run high. Two-thirds of the Central African Republic's 3.8 million people live on less than $1 a day. For Burundi, the figure is only slightly lower at 58 percent. Statistics are not available for the Democratic Republic of Congo where it is apparent that years of civil conflict prevented economic development and exacerbated widespread poverty resulting from the devastating 30-year rule of General Mobutu. Major development issues for the Central Africa region include reconciliation of ethnic conflict, protection of natural resources, repair and improvement of roads and other infrastructure, basic health and education services, and development of the region's considerable economic resources through good governance to serve the needs of the people.

Southern Africa

The region of Southern Africa is comprised of
Angola, Botswana, Lesotho, Malawi, Mozambique,
Namibia, South Africa, Swaziland, Zambia and
Zimbabwe. Because of U.S. media focus on the anti-apartheid
struggle in South Africa from the 1960's to the 1990s, the
region is perhaps the one from which most Americans have
formed their impressions of Africa.

Because of British colonial rule over much of the region, English is widely spoken
in addition to Afrikaans in South Africa and Namibia owing to earlier Dutch
settlement of those areas. The exceptions are Angola and Mozambique, both
former colonies of Portugal, where Portuguese is the official language. Of
course, in each country a variety of indigenous languages are also used like
Shona in Zimbabwe, Xhosa and Zulu in South Africa, Umbundu in Angola,
Chichewa in Malawi and many others.

The region's chief products vary by country. Angola has substantial oil resources
off its Atlantic coast. South Africa is known for its diamonds, gold and other
valuable minerals, while Botswana and Namibia also have substantial deposits
of diamonds plus nickel and other precious metals. Zambia is famed for its
dependence on its copper mines and has suffered economically for the fall in
world demand for this metal. Agricultural products like coffee, tea, tobacco,
sugar, beef and cotton are also widely produced in this heavily agricultural region.

Indigenous religious beliefs dominate in Angola, Botswana and Mozambique,
with Christianity playing a larger role in Malawi, Namibia and Zambia.
In some places, indigenous beliefs are merging with Christian traditions to
create new religious forms. In addition to Christian and traditional religious
practitioners, South Africa has substantial Muslim and Jewish communities.

With 43 million people and the most developed industrial sector in Africa, South Africa dominates the region economically with its relative size, diversity and growing international trade. South Africa provides jobs for workers from a number of surrounding countries. According to the World Bank, less than 2 percent of South Africa's population lives on less than $1 per day although poverty, especially in peri-urban townships and rural areas, remains a significant problem.

By comparison, nearly 64 percent of Zambia's population lives on less than $1 per day. The figure is nearly 42 percent in Malawi, 38 percent in Mozambique, 36 percent in Zimbabwe and 35 percent in Namibia. To foster regional trade and economic growth, the Southern African Development Cooperation Conference (SADCC) was created in 1980, becoming the Southern African Development Community in 1993. Key development issues for the Southern Africa region include the HIV/AIDS pandemic, especially in South Africa and Botswana, the decline of democracy and ongoing economic crises in Zambia and Zimbabwe and regional food security during periods of drought.

East Africa and the Horn

East Africa includes the countries of Kenya, Tanzania and Uganda plus a group of countries, sometimes referred to geographically as the Horn of Africa, including Djibouti, Eritrea, Ethiopia, Somalia and Sudan. The Indian Ocean island nations of Comoros & Mayote, Mauritius, Seychelles, and Madagascar are also included in the East Africa region.

Due to British colonial presence in Kenya, Tanzania and Uganda, English is spoken widely in these countries as well as Swahili and other indigenous languages. English is also spoken among educated classes in Sudan due to British presence there. However, in the Horn of Africa, because of the region's proximity to North Africa and the Arabian Peninsula, Arabic is most commonly used in addition to indigenous languages such as Tigrinya (Eritrea), Amharic, Orominga and Tigrinya (Ethiopia), Nubian (Sudan), Somali (Somalia) and Ganda (Uganda). French colonial outposts resulted in French and a variety of indigenous languages being spoken in Comoros & Mayote, Djibouti, Seychelles and Madagascar. And Italian is still used among older generations in Eritrea, Ethiopia and Somalia because of Italy's historic relationship to those areas.

Islam dominates the Horn of Africa countries of Somalia, Sudan and Djibouti, although Eastern Orthodox Christianity plays a nearly equal role in Ethiopia and Eritrea. Christianity is the principal religion in Kenya and Uganda, while in Tanzania Islam and indigenous religions are more popular.

The region's economic base is overwhelmingly agricultural: coffee and tea in Kenya; coffee and animal hides in Ethiopia; fruits, fish and livestock in Somalia; gum Arabic and cotton in Sudan; and cotton, coffee and tobacco in Uganda and Tanzania. In addition, minerals such as gold, zinc, platinum, copper and uranium are found in the region. Sudan has important oil resources in its southern region, a major factor in that country's 20-year civil war, which may be ending with an agreement on sharing the oil revenues between the dominant northern region and the undeveloped south. Kenya, with its relatively modern economy and proliferation of civil society organizations, is as dependent on its tourism industry for earning foreign exchange as it is on tea and coffee exports.

Ethiopia, linked in the minds of most Americans since the 1980s with famine, is the region's most populous country with nearly 70 million people. Despite the overthrow of a Marxist government and partial settlement of its conflicts in the early 1990s, Ethiopia remains today the region's poorest country. The World Bank estimates that nearly 82 percent of Ethiopia's people live on less than $1 per day, one of the highest rates in the world. By comparison, 23 percent of Kenya's population and 20 percent of Tanzania's population live on less than $1 per day. Somalia's break up and dissolution into clan-based civil war in 1991, following the overthrow of that country's dictator and brief American humanitarian intervention, has continued to cause refugee problems for neighboring Kenya, Ethiopia and Djibouti. The recent clan-agreed framework for ending the conflict and establishing a shared government in the southern and central parts of Somalia could mark the beginning of that country's national rebirth.

The East Africa and Horn region is struggling with democracy, which can hardly be said to exist in Sudan and Somalia. And while the structures of democracy are technically in place in Uganda, Tanzania and Ethiopia, all three countries lack environments conducive to multi-party elections. On the other hand, democracy was given a boost in Kenya when opposition candidate Mwai Kibaki was elected president in 2002. Under Ugandan President Yoweri Mouseveni's regime political parties are barred outright, but Uganda is making significant economic progress and serving as a model to other countries in its successful campaigns to control the spread of HIV/AIDS.

On a regional basis, the leaders of East Africa and the Horn created the Inter-Governmental Authority for Drought and Development (IGADD) in 1986 as a forum for regional security, economic and political issues. The organization also became involved in diplomatic efforts to end the region's numerous civil conflicts, with limited success. Key development issues for the region include improving agricultural production by small-holder farmers; resolving longstanding conflicts in Sudan, Somalia and Uganda as well as between Ethiopia and Eritrea; stopping the HIV/AIDS pandemic; and addressing issues of Islamic fundamentalism and ethnic rivalries within a democratic context.

Appendix III: *Africa Country and Sector Focus of the Foundations and Corporations*

Foundation	Type	Website	Countries in Africa where funds	Sector of funding
American Express	corporate	www.americanexpress.com	South Africa	Education
Bernard Van Leer Foundation	private	www.bernardvanleer.org	Botswana, Egypt, Kenya, Morocco, Mozambique, Namibia, Nigeria, South Africa	Education, Civil Society, Community Development, Healthcare
Carnegie Corporation	private	www.carnegie.org	Botswana, Ghana, Kenya, South Africa, Tanzania, Uganda	Education
Clarence Foundation	public	www.theclarencefoundation.org	Democratic Republic of Congo	Micro-finance
Cogitare Foundation	private	www.cogitarefoundation.org	Mali, Mozambique, South Africa, Zambia	Education
Conrad N. Hilton Foundation	private	www.hiltonfoundation.org	Ethiopia, Ghana, Mali, Nigeria, Niger, Somalia, Sudan, Tanzania	Healthcare, Community Development
Exxon Mobil	corporate	www.exxonmobil.com	Cameroon, Chad, E. Guinea, Kenya, Nigeria	Community Development, Healthcare

Foundation	Type	Website	Countries in Africa where funds	Sector of funding
Family Care Foundation	public	www.familycare.org	Gambia, Ghana, Kenya, Mozambique, Nigeria, Namibia, South Africa, Tanzania, Uganda, Zambia	Education, Healthcare, Community Development, Women's Issues
Firelight Foundation	private	www.firelightfoundation.org	Cameroon, Ethiopia, Kenya, Lesotho, Malawi, Namibia, Rwanda, South Africa, Tanzania, Uganda, Zambia, Zimbabwe	Education, Community Development, Poverty Reduction, Women's Issues
Ford Foundation	private	www.fordfound.org	Ethiopia, Egypt, Ghana, Côte d'Ivoire, Kenya, Mozambique, Namibia, Nigeria, Senegal, South Africa, Tanzania, Tunisia, Uganda, Zimbabwe	Economic Development, Community Development, Human Rights, Peace and Social Justice, Education
Gates Foundation	private	www.gatesfoundation.org	Angola, Ethiopia, Kenya, Malawi, South Africa, Tanzania, Zambia, Zimbabwe	Heathcare
Global Catalyst	corporate	www.global-catalyst.org	Democratic Rep. of Congo, Namibia, Zambia	Education

Foundation	Type	Website	Countries in Africa where funds	Sector of funding
Global Fund for Women	public	www.globalfundforwomen.org	Botswana, Cameroon, Democratic Rep. of Congo, Egypt, Ethiopia, Ghana, Guinea, Kenya, Malawi, Morocco, Mozambique, Nigeria, Somalia, South Africa, Togo, Tanzania, Uganda, Zambia, Zimbabwe	Healthcare, Poverty Reduction, Human Rights, Education, Women's Issues
Global Greengrants Fund	public	www.greengrants.org	Benin, Cameroon, Central African Republic, Chad, Democratic Rep. of Congo, Côte d'Ivoire, Ghana, Kenya, Lesotho, Liberia, Madagascar, Mali, Morocco, Mozambique, Nigeria, Senegal, Somalia, South Africa, Tanzania, Togo, Uganda, Zambia, Zimbabwe	Education, Environmental Issues, Poverty Reduction, Healthcare, Women's Issues
The William and Flora Hewlett Foundation	private	www.hewlett.org	Sudan, Sub-Saharan Regional Programs	Healthcare, Reproductive Health
International Youth Foundation	public	www.iyfnet.org	South Africa	Youth Advocacy

Foundation	Type	Website	Countries in Africa where funds	Sector of funding
Izumi Foundation	public	www.izumi.org	Botswana, Ghana, Kenya, Lesotho, Malawi, Mali, Mozambique, Namibia, Nigeria, South Africa, Swaziland, Tanzania, Uganda, Zambia	Poverty Reduction, Healthcare
J.F. Kapnek	private	www.jfkapnektrust.org	Zimbabwe	HIV Prevention
Kellogg Foundation	private	www.wkkf.org	Botswana, Lesotho, Mozambique, South Africa, Swaziland, Zimbabwe,	Education, Community Development, Poverty Reduction
Kresge Foundation	private	www.kresge.org	Kenya, South Africa	Education
Lawson Valentine Foundation	private	N/A	Burkina Faso	Environmental Justice
MacArthur Foundation	private	www.macfound.org	Kenya, Nigeria, Tanzania, Uganda	Conservation and Sustainable Development, Human Rights, Healthcare, Population, Education
Maidstone Foundation	public	www.maidstonefoundation.org	Tanzania	People with Disabilities
Merck Company Foundation	corporate	www.merck.com	Botswana	HIV Prevention/ Treatment
McKnight Foundation	private	www.mcknight.org	Tanzania, Uganda, Zimbabwe	Women's Empowerment

APPENDIX III: AFRICA COUNTRY AND SECTOR FOCUS OF THE FOUNDATIONS AND CORPORATIONS

Foundation	Type	Website	Countries in Africa where funds	Sector of funding
Mott Foundation	private	www.mott.org	South Africa	Citizen Rights, Race and Ethnic Relations, Nonprofit Sector
Mulago Foundation	private	N/A	Kenya	Community Development
Packard Foundation	private	www.packard.org	Ethiopia, Nigeria	Population Growth
Open Society	private	www.soros.org	Egypt, Mozambique, South Africa	Education, Human Rights, Law and Justice, Women's Issues
Rockefeller Foundation	private	www.rockfound.org	Ethiopia, Kenya, Senegal, South Africa, Uganda, Zimbabwe	Education, Arts and Culture, Environmental Law, Healthcare, Women's Issues, Information
Rockefeller Brothers Fund	private	www.rbf.org	South Africa	Education, Orphans and Vulnerable Children
Trinity Grants Program	church	www.trinitywallstreet.org	Democratic Rep. of Congo, Ghana, Kenya, Madagascar, Nigeria, Rwanda, South Africa, Sudan, Tanzania, Uganda, Zambia, Zimbabwe,	Education, Community Development, Primary & Preventative Healthcare, Peace Building, Leadership and Management Training

Foundation	Type	Website	Countries in Africa where funds	Sector of funding
U.N. Foundation	public	www.unfoundation.org	Angola, Benin, Botswana, Burkina Faso, Cameroon, Chad, Democratic Rep. of Congo, Egypt, Ethiopia, Gambia, Ghana, Kenya, Lesotho, Madagascar, Malawi, Mali, Morocco, Mozambique, Niger, Nigeria, Rwanda, Senegal, Sierra Leone, Somalia, South Africa, Sudan, Swaziland, Tanzania, Togo, Tunisia, Uganda, Zambia, Zimbabwe	Women & Population, Environment, Peace, Security, Human Rights, Healthcare

Appendix IV: *Africa At A Glance*[*]

Number of Countries:	53
Largest Country By Area:	Sudan (size of U.S. east of the Mississippi River)
Most Populous Country:	Nigeria (size of Texas, Oklahoma and Louisiana combined)
Newest Countries:	Namibia (1990, size of Texas) Eritrea (1993, size of Kentucky)
Population:	876.9 million
Urban Population (sub-Saharan):	36.4%
Population Under 15 (2003 figure):	43%
Most Populous Countries:	Nigeria (130 million) Ethiopia (66 million, three times the size of California)
Least Populous Countries:	Sao Tome & Principe (151,000, one-third the size of Rhode Island) Cape Verde (446,000, three-quarters the size of Delaware)
Life Expectancy:	50 average 35 in Botswana 74 in Mauritius, Seychelles and Tunisia
Population Living on Less than $1 per day (2003 figure):	49% average 73% in Mali <2% in South Africa, Algeria, Egypt and Tunisia

**Population with Sustainable
Access to an Improved
Water Source:**   100% in Mauritius

                            29% in Somalia

Economic Growth Rate: 1.9% average annual growth for 2000–2004

                            40% in Cape Verde

                            6.2% in Zimbabwe

Literacy Rates: 53% average for women (2003 figure)

                            92% in the Seychelles

                            12% in Mali

                            71% average for men (2003 figure)

                            93% in Equatorial Guinea

                            43% in Mali

Infant Mortality Rate: 137.6 per 1,000 live births

                            282.8 per 1,000 in Sierra Leone

                            13.5 per 1,000 in the Seychelles

**Estimated Population
Living with HIV/AIDS
in sub-Saharan Africa:**   24.5 million

                            5.5 million in South Africa

*Figures are combined from *African Development Indicators 2006* by the World Bank, Country Profile Table from the World Bank (devdata.worldbank.org), the United Nations Population Fund (www.unfpa.org) and the Lazarus Foundation (www.lazarusfoundation.com). Where 2003 figures are provided, data was taken from African Development Indicators 2003 by the World Bank.

About the Authors

Rob Buchanan is director of international programs at the Council on Foundations in Washington, D.C. Rob's previous experience includes 10 years with Oxfam America, serving for five years as program director for the Horn of Africa and subsequently as the organization's Washington representative for policy and advocacy. In addition, Rob served on the staffs of the United States Senate and House of Representatives in foreign policy positions. He also worked on global environmental and development issues for EarthAction, leading a campaign that resulted in U.S. Senate ratification of the United Nations Convention to Combat Desertification. Rob is a graduate of The Johns Hopkins University and earned a Master of Arts degree in International Relations from The Johns Hopkins School of Advanced International Studies.

Jayne Booker's professional life has focused on sustainable economic development, primarily in Africa. After serving as a Peace Corps volunteer in Benin, Jayne went on to pursue her passion for international development with Coopers & Lybrand, then Deloitte & Touche. Her last position with Deloitte & Touche was as managing director, international lending agency services, based in Johannesburg, South Africa, where she lived from 1994 to 1999. This group provided economic development consulting services throughout Africa to both government and nongovernmental entities. In 1999, Jayne joined the David and Lucile Packard Foundation as a program officer in the Organizational Effectiveness Program where she was responsible for supporting grantees of the foundation's Population Program by recommending and providing capacity-building grants. As co-chair of the Africa Grantmakers' Affinity Group (AGAG), she helped nurture the group through its start-up phase. Jayne now works as an executive director for a Silicon Valley nonprofit and does consulting work with other foundations and nonprofits. She holds a Bachelor of Arts degree in History from Duke University and a Master of Business Administration degree from the University of North Carolina.